Photo: Sean Brady

P R A I S E   F O R   P A R K   R A N G E R

"... Muleady-Mecham chronicles with refreshing honesty some of the more hair-raising experiences (of being a Park Ranger)... The lay public will be nothing short of stunned, fellow Park Service folks in non-ranger fields will be enlightened, and even veteran Rangers will read her stories with an attitude of respect... *Park Ranger* is a terrific read and an exciting one too. Through it all, Muleady-Mecham takes us with her, writing with a style that keeps readers on the edge of their seats while at the same time celebrates the grand majesty of the landscapes in which the events unfold."

– Kevin Moses, Association of National Park Rangers

"If you've ever wondered about the details behind the Ranger's Log entries, then pick up this engagingly-written, fast-paced account of life as a Protection Ranger. Muleady-Mecham's name is a familiar one at Grand Canyon National Park, but her experience as a Protection Ranger has also taken her to Sequoia and Kings Canyon in California, Everglades National Park in Florida, California's Death Valley, the U.S.S. Arizona Memorial at Pearl Harbor and Blue Ridge Parkway in North Carolina's Great Smoky Mountains. Her book is not only the story of her experiences through rescues, recoveries, arrests and myriad other emergencies – it tells the stories of all of those who work behind the scenes to, as Muleady-Mecham says, put the "Service" in "National Park Service.""

– Williams-Grand Canyon News

"Nancy is a very skilled Ranger who writes of her fascinating real-life adventures as a modern-day professional National Park Ranger. You won't believe what is going on behind the scenes of your peaceful visit to a National Park. An informative read for those who may be considering a career as a Park Ranger or who are simply interested in the work of these talented people. A great procedural refresher for those in the profession wishing to brush up on medical emergency and law enforcement response."

– Jack Davis, Associate Director, National Park Service (retired)

"Ever dreamed of a career as a Park Ranger? Nancy Muleady-Mecham goes beyond campfire talks and nifty uniforms to show us the gritty reality of rangerdom. A few hair-raising anecdotes from her 20-plus years of rangering include performing a field amputation, saving a 17-year-old heart attack victim, and dealing with a lost man, a shooting, a burning car and a head injury in the space of a single day. Maybe being an accountant isn't so bad."

– High Country News

"This book is a collection of stories that's a must-read for park visitors, some who might find themselves in life-threatening situations and relying on the resourcefulness of a Park Ranger."

– Arizona Daily Sun

"Adrenaline junkies, this is a book for you. This compilation of short vignettes is an informative group of experiences of the author during her service career within many of America's National Parks … as detailed in this book through her recounting of notable events experienced, she skillfully illustrated that training is very important to be a successful Park Ranger. This book details how the author put all of her training to use at one point or another during her tenure as a NPS Ranger. The one thing that becomes immediately apparent is that being a Park Ranger is not even close to being routine. Depending on the season, the location, staffing levels and the fate of the gods, a Park Ranger must be able to do many things. Situations can occur requiring the Ranger to also be a fireman, a tour guide, a search and rescue team member, an EMT, a naturalist and/or just a friend; sometimes more than one thing at once. Multitasking is definitely the word of the day. This book is extremely enjoyable and I found myself compelled to keep turning the page to find out if the events would end successfully."

– J.M. De Santis, Drug Enforcement Agent, The Eighteen Eleven

"Forget campfire talks and Smokey the Bear. The real-life world of a modern-day National Park Service Ranger is nothing like you've ever imagined. Nancy Muleady-Mecham, a veteran NPS Ranger, takes you on a wild, revealing and sometimes shocking journey into the realities of this world."

– Tom Myers, coauthor of *Over The Edge: Death in Grand Canyon*

"Jessica is a senior home-schooled student, and a Senior Girl Scout who has earned Girl Scouting's highest award, the Gold Award . . . . Last September we visited the Southwest (we live in Georgia) . . . In Kolb Studio, she saw your book. What immediately appealed to her was the picture on the front cover, a female park ranger on horseback! I bought the book for her, and she scarcely put it down until she had read it completely. I've read it too, and thoroughly enjoyed it.

After reading your book, she has decided that if vet school doesn't work out for her, she would like to consider the Park Service, as a backcountry ranger. You have provided her an excellent example of a strong, positive female role model, something that Girl Scout leaders try so hard to provide for their Scouts. She has some experience with climbing and rappelling, canoeing, hiking, and backpacking, and could identify with several of the skills you talked about in your book."

— **Donna Barrett, Troop Leader, Senior Girl Scout Troop 3417, and Jessica's mom**

"*Park Ranger* by Nancy Muleady-Mecham is as much a treat to review as it is to read. The author, who is a skilled paramedic and nurse as well as a skilled firefighter, writes in an accessible but sophisticated style that makes reading a pleasure."

— **The Protection Ranger**

"This is a wonderful depiction of life with the National Park Service, from training to working as a Law Enforcement Officer, paramedic, naturalist, and firefighter. The stories are exciting, humorous, and amazing accounts of what it is like to be a ranger. (It) keeps you turning the pages to see what could possibly happen next. Definitely recommended for those interested in the Park Service as a career!"

— **Emily Mount, Park Ranger Naturalist**

"Not only is Ranger Nancy a paramedic, an RN, a teacher, a firefighter, a cop, a swiftwater rescuer, a marksman, an artist, a friend and a wife, she's quite a storyteller, as well.

Oh, the images she paints for her readers! I could feel the heat of the flames, the chill of the October night on the desert, and I swear I gasped as I looked over the rim to see the body on the ledge, 400 feet below. Ranger Nancy makes me wish I'd been a Park Ranger, too!"

— **Kathleen Day, RN**

"I loved this book. The stories are riveting. I'm an avid backpacker; I find myself reflecting on this book while I'm in the backcountry.

I usually have a short attention span, but I was captivated by the variety of situations and stories. One thing that I really enjoy is how the author assumes that you're intelligent enough to want to know what's going on in the different medical situations. Most books that I pick up these days don't appeal to people that want to educate themselves; if you have any interest in medicine, the outdoors, adventure or interesting people, buy this book. Dr. Nancy Eileen Muleady-Mecham is one of those people that makes you wonder, "How can one person do all that?" If you've ever visited a National Park, you may or may not realize what these people do behind the scenes. They're expected to be protectors of our resources, law enforcement, firefighters, medical technicians, and experts on the local environment. If you've ever gotten into trouble in the back-country, you know these people are angels. They love their job and they have the best office in the whole world. There's not a lot of books out there that give you real insight on what goes on in a National Park; this is the one to get. After reading this book, I have more respect than ever for what the rangers do. Dr. Muleady-Mecham is at the head of her class. If you know any young people that are considering a future in the National Park Service (or aren't sure what they want to be) – BUY THEM THIS BOOK!!"

– Greg Brush, Captain, Structural Fire, Xanterra Parks and Recreation

"I have been a second-career park ranger for the past 17 years, working in federal, county and state park agencies, and even before that, since 1971, a wilderness search and rescue volunteer. I am a 30-year-plus EMT and was a paramedic for a while. I just wish I could have put it all down on paper as well as "Ranger Nancy" has in this excellent book. This book captures the exhilaration of hanging at the end of a short-haul line, or taking that first step over a cliff on a rappel rope; the aggravation of dealing with crowds and drunks and the hope of doing everything you can to save a life, and having it work just when that hope seems lost. It is both magnificent and gut wrenching, and Nancy relays it in great, highly readable prose. The author is a ranger, Critical Care RN, Paramedic, rescue specialist and has both Masters and Ph.D.s on her resume, yet I never felt she was talking down to the reader. Ranger Nancy's stories are the real deal and, like many of us, she obviously loves the work. She takes you with her on ambulance and rescue calls, murder and mayhem, and makes you feel like you are there. When she told the story of the murder of Ranger Joe on the Blue Ridge Parkway, and his wife having to clear the parking lot so the helicopter could land to take him to the trauma center, I had tears in my eyes and a big lump in my throat.... Because of her extensive medical training, there is a lot of detail on the EMS and rescue part of being a ranger, but that makes for good reading for EMTs and medics, too. This rates as one of the two best books I have read about being a Park Ranger ... well done, Ms. Muleady-Mecham!"

– Snow Ranger, Courtesy of *Amazon.com, Inc* or its affiliates. All rights reserved.

"If you'd like to learn more about the world of park medics, pick up a copy of Nancy Muleady-Mecham's new book, *Park Ranger.* Nancy has worked for more than twenty years as a Ranger, not only at Sequoia and Kings Canyon, but also at Death Valley and Grand Canyon, and her stories of rescues and lives saved will give you a clear window into what Park Rangers face in their work."

– William Tweed, Chief Park Naturalist, SEKI (retired)

"I have read it *(Park Ranger)* cover to cover and loved it all. I think it is a superb book in that it is personal, but also makes really clear what a Protection Ranger really has to deal with on a regular and recurring basis ... and indirectly, what kind of training is required to do it. It is a book that every member and their staff on the NPS appropriations and authorizing committees in the House and Senate should read – not to mention all of the leaders of the NPS. I will reference it often to those kinds of people .... Thank you for writing this great book, and for being the fabulous ranger that you obviously were. I am sorry I did not know you throughout your career ... it is you folks who are the reputation and heart of the NPS. My gratitude cannot be adequately expressed, but I tried to live my career for all you folks and for the people who come to the parks."

– John Reynolds, Deputy Director, National Park Service (retired)

PARK RANGER
SEQUEL

MORE TRUE STORIES FROM A RANGER'S
CAREER IN AMERICA'S NATIONAL PARKS

Nancy Eileen Muleady-Mecham

VTP
Vishnu Temple Press • Flagstaff, AZ

ISBN 0-9795055-2-6
ISBN 978-0-9795055-2-2
LCCN 2007943645

Front cover photo from the personal collection of Nancy Muleady-Mecham
Back cover author photograph: Sean Brady
Cover design and book layout: Sandra Kim Muleady
All other photos are from the author's personal collection unless otherwise noted.

Vishnu Temple Press, LLC
P.O. Box 30821
Flagstaff, AZ 86003-0821
www.vishnutemplepress.com

PRINTED IN THE UNITED STATES

For Mom, Eileen Shelley Muleady

For Kathleen Marie Muleady Seager

And For Shannon

CONTENTS

ACKNOWLEDGEMENTS

The success of Park Ranger *was personally satisfying. It is in its third printing. Since its debut, I learned of the many people who love our National Parks and enjoyed reading adventure stories. I wrote those stories because my family and friends encouraged me to do so. When* Park Ranger *went into its second printing, my publisher, Hazel Clark, of Vishnu Temple Press, was very supportive and said, "Start working on a sequel." Tom Martin, also of Vishnu Temple Press, was my Physical Therapist and literally helped me to get back on my feet again. Special thanks go to Dr. Timothy Bonatus for making me bionic, and Dr. Tom Myers for his friendship. Thanks again to Sean Brady for great photos.*

My family and friends deserve special mention. Their enthusiasm buoyed my confidence and allowed me to undertake this second huge venture. Sadly, my sister Kathleen died before seeing the stories in print, but she heard all of them. Shannon, my beloved, noodle-headed and loving Golden Retriever died of cancer, but lives on in our hearts. My husband Kent read the manuscript and gave great suggestions and is always there for me. Dr. Kris Justus did another magnificent job of editing. Sandra Kim Muleady continues to impress me with her graphic design skills. Sandy's ability to add the right touches to a page design or outlook to the cover is amazing. My best friend, Mary Anne Carlton, let me bounce ideas and stories off of her and encouraged me the entire time. Special thanks go to the gifted author, Tony Hillerman, for his kind words. Judge Stephen Verkamp also added wonderful words, and he was always fair when I appeared before him in court to testify. My mom, Eileen Shelley Muleady, has always been the source of my strength and inspiration. I know she is smilin' from above.

INTRODUCTION

This second book of stories from my career as a Ranger is a bit different from the first. I received many inquiries about "me" after the release of *Park Ranger*. What was my life like beyond a Ranger's life? I have lifted the veil slightly to allow a peek or two. In addition, there were many shorter stories I wanted to share. I called them vignettes throughout the preparation. They are spread throughout the book among the longer stories.

These last seven years have brought tremendous change to my life. With time and age comes loss and sorrow. I also have had more opportunities. I hope these stories bring as much thought, provocation, fun, and reality to the reader as they did to me as I lived them.

Nancy E. Muleady-Mecham
Grand Canyon, AZ 2008

Carnegie Hall

■ Death Valley, California

The second week in November is the focus of great attention in Death Valley. It's called 49er week, and started as a celebration of the first crossing of the valley by non-Indians in 1849. It has evolved into a gala that includes art shows, gold panning, fiddler contests and more. Thousands of people in thousands of recreational vehicles, tents, and campers come to revel in the beautiful fall weather, sunny skies and crisp nights.

When I saw my first 49er encampment, the sheer number of people mesmerized me. Sunset Campground looked like an RV back lot with row upon row of motorhomes lined up into the distance. Furnace Creek Campground overflowed into the desert. No one was turned away and the impact took its toll on the fragile environment as well as the Ranger staff.

Early in my career as a seasonal Ranger Naturalist at Death Valley, I developed a living history character named Juliet Brier, a woman among the 1849ers who crossed Death Valley. I wore a gingham dress and apron, old shoes, and a bonnet, and was ready to present my character to the twenty or so visitors who might be interested in my interpretation. As I hid behind some mesquite trees near the back of the auditorium, Larry, a fellow Naturalist, came careening around the corner out of breath.

"You'll have to move your program inside of the auditorium," he said.

"Are you kidding... its supposed to be 1849. How do I explain away a huge building in the middle of Death Valley? I want to encounter my audience in the serenity of the desert," I replied.

"Nancy, you have more than 200 people ready to see Juliet Brier. We will need a microphone and crowd control," Larry responded.

I was shocked. It was 10:00 a.m. in the morning on a weekday. This was the first presentation of a living history character in Death Valley and I suppose its uniqueness drew a crowd. After agreeing to try it without a microphone, Larry and others herded the visitors into the auditorium and counted over 270 attendees. I entered, stumbled a bit at first, and then got into character, telling of my crossing of the valley with the other 49ers in winter. It was a hit and while I loved the character, I never did get used to giving the re-enactment in the auditorium. We had hundreds at each program.

A few years later, I was no longer a Naturalist/Interpreter Ranger at Death Valley, but a seasonal Protection Ranger. I was assigned to Stovepipe Wells, the area adjacent to the sand dunes and away from the congestion of the more popular Furnace Creek. The area Ranger, Roger, had left recently for another position back east, but he and I had finished the work on the campground before he left and so it was now ready for the 49er encampment in November. The only permanent Ranger assigned to Stovepipe Wells was Russ. Russ was always on the cutting edge of new technology, buying new computers, radios, etc. He had a wife and children and, like all of the other Park Service employees at Stovepipe Wells, paid rent and utilities for a government trailer. His was a doublewide and mine was a single. Owing to the exposure to hot summers, cold winters and innumerable sand storms, the housing was considered by most of us something to be condemned.

But I was happy with my little trailer, especially since I did not have to share it. I duct-taped the windows and the opening for the evaporative cooler to try to keep out the sand when the wind blew. It was my sanctuary. After a day on the road, hiking up a side canyon or talking to hundreds of visitors, it was nice to have an escape. But that didn't always work. One evening, I was working a night shift and had come home to make dinner. I had taken my gun belt off and had placed it with my radio on a chair in the main room. I was cooking over a skillet when the door burst open. In jumped Dan, a maintenance worker. He was out of breath, grasping the door handle and pushing the door open to its limit.

He looked at me, looked at my equipment on the chair and said, "Get your sh— together, Nancy; there's been a big accident on Daylight Pass and we need you to respond."

Who needs a phone when you've got a Dan?

My first 49ers as a Protection Ranger at Stovepipe Wells started early. On Wednesday in the early afternoon we received a report of a rollover motor vehicle accident with occupants ejected from the vehicle. I raced up the hill to Wildrose in my patrol car and Russ came with the ambulance. The Wildrose Ranger, also named Nancy, was en route. A white sedan was poised on its rear bumper upside down with its nose in the air on an embankment on a curve. The skid marks on the road were glistening with newness and bystanders were crouched beside the two patients, a good 100 feet from the car. Going at a speed far greater than the curve could handle, they had flipped the sedan end over end and around in a circle. One had been ejected because he wasn't wearing a seatbelt. They were a mess. The Flight for Life helicopter and a ground ambulance were both called because the chopper could only take one patient. One patient was a 47-year-old male who was disoriented and seemed dazed. One of the first lay persons on scene said he had witnessed the patient having a seizure. This could be a sign of a severe internal head injury. He was bleeding profusely from a laceration to his head that nearly scalped him, and had lots of bumps and bruises and road rash. He also had diminished sounds to his left chest cavity, indicating a pneumothorax or collapsed lung. The second patient was a 55-year-old male who was also disoriented and, according to those first on scene, was unconscious for quite awhile. He could tell me his name, but that was about all. His face was ground hamburger and he had trouble speaking because of the facial trauma. He also had many other injuries and bruising to the rest of his body. We splinted fractures, immobilized spinal columns, started IV fluids and placed both of them on oxygen. As one went by ground and the other by helicopter, we shook our collective heads, wondering if either would make it through the multisystem trauma they had suffered. It could all have been so easily avoided if they had worn their seatbelts and slowed down.

The next day was Friday and the big weekend was upon us. There were hundreds of people in the Stovepipe Wells area and two Rangers, Russ and me. At 8:10 a.m., as I approached the Ranger Station (one room in a two-room little shack), I noticed a 68-year-old female who was standing in a line. She didn't look well to me and as I walked up to her to ask if she was okay, she began to collapse. I caught her and helped her the rest of the way to the ground. I radioed to Russ to bring the ambulance and turned my attention to Katherine, the patient.

Katherine was from Tucson and was pale and sweaty, but with the program. (I once learned to say, "Horses sweat, men perspire, women glow," so I guess Katherine was "glowing.") It turned out she had a history of near-syncopal episodes, almost passing out, for the past sixty years! She just stood in line too long without breakfast. After she was checked out medically and found to be all right, she was treated and released. I went to complete the paperwork while Russ returned the ambulance to its shed.

I finally had a chance to get on the road, but was called back to the Ranger Station just after 11:00 a.m. for a report of a burned hand. Ruby, a small 78-year-old lady, was sitting in consternation as I arrived. She had too much to do to hang out here, she exclaimed. Apparently, this near-octogenarian slipped and put her hand on the hot muffler of her dune buggy and suffered a second-degree burn. The blister was intact and, after checking her vital signs and cleaning her hand, I sent Ruby on her way.

The rest of the shift was busy but uneventful. I finally retreated to my trailer after 6:00 p.m., changed my clothes, had dinner and then headed out to be a civilian among the 49er festivities. I saw Russ and his wife Cheryl at the art tables and strolled out to the front of the Ranger Station area to listen to the Liar's Contest. This was always great fun. Those who could tell tall tales and twist a story as if caught in a typhoon took turns telling the best, almost not really-true tale. There was laughter and incredulity and guffaws at punch lines.

About ten minutes before eight in the evening, Delbert, a lively 75-year-old Liars Contest regular, was up doing his best to one-up the previous storytellers. He wove his tale and hooked us, and was drawing us in toward the end of his tale when he took a breath. We all hung forward for the punch line as he smiled, leaned forward . . . and just kept on going. He face-planted right on the five-foot by five-foot square stage. Of the 400 or so people in the audience, most weren't sure what to do. Then applause began as, in some confusion, they thought the fall was the punch line. I knew better.

I was 15 feet from the stage when he fell and jumped up onto the small elevation. Someone had already turned him over and was trying to give him chest compressions. He was out cold. I yelled, "Wait!" and felt for a carotid pulse. In some film presentations on TV and in the movies, it always irritates me when I see someone who, in theory should know better, put their thumb or fingers on the side of the patient's neck to feel for a pulse. The only thing they can feel there is skin and muscle! First, your thumb already has a pretty good pulse compared to your fingers and should not be used to find a pulse. You could mistake your thumb's pulse for the patient's. Secondly, the carotid artery is very close to the trachea or windpipe. You merely put two of your fingers on the middle of the patient's trachea and slide them to the side to a groove where the carotid artery's pulse can be felt – if there is one to feel. In this case, Delbert had a weak pulse of about 40 beats per minute. But his breathing was very irregular; I sensed an inspiration every 15 seconds or longer. It was shallow and short; what we call agonal or last breaths.

I looked up to see Russ and asked for the ambulance and the heart monitor. He took off as Delbert began one pitiful last breath, and then no more. I did not have my EMS bag. I did not have my key ring with the pocket shield in it. Everyone knew I was the Stovepipe Wells Ranger and paramedic and I felt 400 sets of eyes on me. Talk about peer pressure. I didn't feel I could wait for Russ' return, so I tilted Delbert's head back to open his airway as I lifted his chin. I looked, listened and felt. There was still no breath. It was inevitable. I lip-locked.

I pinched his nose with my left thumb and forefinger as I tilted his head back to open his airway. I placed my mouth over his partially open mouth and, with a deep breath, I began artificial respirations, also known as mouth-to-mouth. I felt uncomfortable because I was used to training with a barrier to separate the patient's body fluids from getting into my mouth, but here I had no choice. He still had a weak pulse as I continued rescue breathing. No one in the audience moved. I asked for room around me and for someone to bring the oxygen from the Ranger Station less than 100 feet away. It seemed like a very long time, but Russ was back in less than four minutes with all of the advanced cardiac life support equipment.

We put an OPA (orapharangeal airway) into Delbert's mouth to pull the tongue from the back of the throat or pharynx so it would not block the flow of oxygen. Russ then hooked the bag-valve mask to oxygen and took over rescue breathing from me. Cheryl, Russ' wife, said Rangers Liudyte and Joe were responding to help from the Furnace Creek area.

I took a quick look with the paddles from the LifePak 5, an

older and earlier model of more modern monitor/defibrillators. You could read a patient's EKG or heart rhythm by hooking the leads (cables) to the patient and defibrillating them as needed by sending a shock of electricity through the paddles. In a hurry though, you didn't need the cables right away. You could hold the paddles to the patient's chest and read the rhythm through the paddles and then shock immediately. This was called a quick look and saved the time of putting the leads on. Once a shock was not indicated, the cables were put in place. Today, we don't often use paddles anymore, but safer remote defibrillation pads.

* * * *

I'll never forget the very first time I defibrillated a patient. I was a paramedic student in the San Francisco Bay area. I was going to the Stanford University Hospital Paramedic School and had completed my didactic (classroom) section and in-hospital (clinical) section, and was now doing my required ride-a-long section. I had been assigned to an ambulance from a fire station in San Carlos off Interstate 101. My preceptor was Larry and his partner was Ron. As a student, I got to check out the ambulance, scrub it inside and out, be ready to answer any medical questions at anytime from them and, generally, be treated as a rookie. The first few calls were very minor and my role was to watch Larry and Ron to see how paramedic teams work together. Then I would take the lead on calls and Larry would watch my every move to make sure I knew what I was doing, as well as to teach me how things were done.

The very best part of the assignment was where I stayed at the fire station. It was an older station with two floors. The firemen and medics all worked 24-hour shifts. Among them, I was the only woman on that shift. The sleeping arrangements downstairs did not take mixed gender teams into account, so I was told I would be sleeping upstairs. I was taken up a set of metal stairs to a wide open room with a row of beds along the wall, no doubt from a time when there was more money for more firefighters. I was shown the bathroom around the corner and the brass pole I would be using to slide down to the ambulance bay. Whoo! Hoo! That just does not happen anymore; with people landing on each other and twisting ankles, they were not considered safe and were being phased out. I was one of the last to be able to partake of this wonderful tradition.

After a fairly calm night of two calls, I went upstairs to my private floor. I had my jumpsuit at the ready; my belt with my tool holster, radio holster and stethoscope were on the railing next to the pole. My boots were unlaced and at my bedside. I am a very light sleeper and can wake up instantly. So when the alarm went off at 3:03 a.m., I jumped out of bed and into my jumpsuit, slipped my boots on, grabbed my holster belt and slid down the pole. I entered the side of the ambulance and sat in the jump seat behind the driver's compartment and put on my seatbelt. That was where all the rookie students sat. I checked my penlight, put my belt on and waited for Larry and Ron to climb aboard. The call came in for an "unconscious man." At that we joked, "What else do you expect in the middle of the night?"

We ran with full lights but no sirens, due to the lack of traffic and the early hour. There was a fog hanging overhead as we raced toward Belmont, a nearby city. As we pulled up behind the fire engine, the dispatcher updated the call to "Code Blue – Full Arrest." Yikes! A Code Blue meant a person with no heartbeat or respirations. This was to be the first call I was to take the lead on.

I grabbed the heart monitor/defibrillator, Ron grabbed the radio and Larry the drug and airway box. I looked up at a long flight of brick steps to the entrance of the home and began the climb. Instantly, I realized I had made a blunder. In all of that time waiting for Ron and Larry and driving to the call, I never tied my boots! I "clumped, clumped, clumped" up the steps as my feet would partially slide out of my boots with each step. "What a noodlehead!" I said to myself and hoped no one noticed.

We entered the house. It was warmer than the foggy night and a light blue shag carpet suppressed the sounds of my slipping boots. Down a hall and up a flight of stairs, we took a right turn into a bedroom. The double bed was pushed back against the wall and firemen were on the floor performing CPR on a 62-year-old man. There was a scar down the front of his chest where the compressions were being done. Past bypass surgery, I thought, and another fireman with a bag-valve-mask was breathing air into the patient's lungs. The patient was naked, except for an afghan someone had thrown over his genitals. I was told the patient had risen to go to the bathroom then fell onto the bed, moaning. His wife called 911 immediately and the firemen were on scene in seven minutes. They had moved him from the bed to the floor where CPR would be more effective.

Larry got right to work securing an advanced airway. My job was the heart. I quickly placed the EKG paddles onto the patient's chest and saw ventricular fibrillation (V Fib). I knew that he needed to be defibrillated, but I had never been in charge before. I had never shocked a real person before, only a mannequin. Larry was busy so I looked over to Ron and said, "Shock him, right?"

Ron said "Yep."

So I got out the conducting gel and squeezed a good amount on the left paddle and rubbed the paddles together. The paddles were plastic rectangles with metal pads on the bottom. They were attached to the defibrillator by thick, plastic-coated coiled wires. When I set the energy output and charged the defibrillator, nothing happened. Yikes. I immediately thought I had messed something up. Ron reached down and tried and confirmed the battery was dead. *Phew.* We continued CPR as a fireman ran out to the ambulance to get a backup battery. We quickly replaced the cold dead battery with a fresh one and charged again. This time I pressed one paddle to the right side of the patient's chest and one on his side below his left armpit.

"Clear," I said three times as I looked around the patient to be sure everyone was clear of contact with him. Then I shocked him. There was a slight twitch to his chest muscle, but no large zapping sound like TV. I wasn't sure I had done it correctly, but the screen showed a power discharge and a return to V Fib. I looked at Ron and said, "Shock again?" and again he said, "Yep," with the tone of a patient, experienced paramedic bemused at a rookies' newness.

After charging the defibrillator, I looked over at the screen to confirm the rhythm. Again I called "Clear," and looked around. You are supposed to apply about 25 pounds of pressure during defibrillation. I must have taken some pressure off of the paddles that I had pressed tightly to his chest because the next thing I knew, an arc of blue electricity streaked across the patient's chest, singing his chest hairs along the way. The smell of burning hair was so distinctive. I was aghast until I looked at the monitor. There was a rhythm.

"Well, I'll be damned," Larry said, as he too saw the

functional rhythm on the monitor. Soon, the patient, Tom, began to breathe on his own and then moan. His blood pressure climbed to 126/92 with a steady pulse of 80. I started an IV as Ron went to get the gurney. Larry completed the call to the Base Station Physician and we pushed the drugs to keep the patient going.

The firemen helped carry Tom downstairs on the gurney and, at the bottom of the stairs, two older women were clasped in each other's arms. I walked up and said, "He is breathing on his own and he has a heart beat." They stared at me and one said, "Really?" They rushed to get their jackets to go to the hospital.

We went to Chope Hospital where the patient was placed in the ICU and did survive. He had a history of strokes and triple bypass surgery. It just wasn't his time tonight . . . not with early CPR and defibrillation and field medications. I was walking on air – much easier now since I had tied my boots.

* * * *

At Stovepipe Wells with Delbert, I again saw the familiar V Fib pattern on the monitor. I gelled up the paddles and called out "Clear," admonishing people to not touch the patient, lest they get shocked with 300 joules of energy. It's enough energy to restart or stop any heart. I defibrillated Delbert, a now familiar soundless procedure with the accompanying chest contraction, but the new rhythm was a heart breaker. It was asystole or flat-line. Once you see asystole, the chances of getting that heart going again plummet. There is no electrical rhythm coming from the heart, nothing to defibrillate. Today, we might have tried an external pacemaker on an asystolic heart, but not back then.

I ordered CPR to resume and pulled up his shirtsleeve. I started an IV in his right antecubital (AC) vein. I began pushing the drugs on the protocol list: epinephrine, atropine, lidocaine sodium bicarbonate, at the precise dosages and intervals and with circulation of the drugs with CPR. I went to Delbert's head and placed an endotracheal tube (an advanced airway) in his throat through his vocal cords.

We worked hard on that stage for 45 minutes, but there was no sign of life to his heart or his person. It's kind of strange, but when we are working a full code, I can often tell whether there is "something" to work toward or if we are going through the motions on a body where life has fled. To me, it felt as if Delbert had been gone from the beginning.

Joe and Liudyte arrived toward the end of our efforts. I contacted the Base Station Physician through the radio system while Joe continued the Advanced Life Support (ALS) efforts. I spoke to the physician and relayed all of our efforts and the flat line on the monitor. The physician decided that despite our efforts, Delbert was indeed gone and called the code, pronouncing him dead at 10:35 p.m. I asked Dispatch to cancel the Flight For Life helicopter and to call the Inyo County Coroner.

We stopped CPR and I thanked everyone for their help. We were very sad on the stage, but the audience was devastated. This was real life in front of them and it did not have a happy ending. People shuffled away in small groups with low murmurs of conversation. I sat back on my knees and looked at them, turning my head all around, losing sight of them as they walked away from the lights' reach. I felt like I had let them all down. I know I did my best and that is just the way it is, but it was still very sad.

We needed permission from the coroner to move the body.

Once we received it, we placed Delbert on the gurney in the back of the ambulance and took him up to the ambulance bay to wait for the coroner.

The following November, I found myself living and working at Furnace Creek. They wanted a paramedic assigned to the busiest area of the park. The 49er Encampment was upon us again with even more RVs, tents, cars and people squeezed into the saltpan of the surrounding area. The interesting thing about working Death Valley in the winter season is the sheer numbers of older and elderly people who come. It's warmer; many retired folks just enjoy the desert. And not only do they enjoy it, but they are passionate to learn about it. I would have folks come to my geology talks, take notes and then, finding me later, compare an alluvial fan they had discovered to the points in my presentation. It was very rewarding. We all realize getting older can take its toll on a person's health. The number of elderly caused the medical calls to climb through the roof in Death Valley in winter, especially during the 49er Encampment. This year's gathering was no exception.

On Thursday, a 58-year-old male had a sudden onset of left upper area chest pain for 30 minutes while working at the filling station. Bill described his pain as excruciating, but not like his past angina or quintuple bypass surgery. He was hypertensive with a blood pressure of 190/90. He was short of breath (SOB), his heart looked good on the monitor and his lungs were clear, but he did have swollen ankles with pitting edema. When this occurs, you can push a finger into the swollen area of the lower leg and the area will blanch, sometimes not regaining color or rebounding for several seconds. This could be a sign of right-sided heart failure.

After starting an IV and placing him on oxygen, I contacted the Base Station Physician in Las Vegas and received orders for nitroglycerin followed by morphine, as needed. As we headed to meet the Flight For Life helicopter, Bill said he felt better and was flown out of the valley to the ER.

The next day at noon, I was called to Sunset Campground overflow to an RV with a 63-year-old female complaining of abdominal pain and total body ache. Madeline had a history of kidney problems, bladder infections, vomiting and diarrhea. It sounded like a nasty gastrointestinal bug. Her urine was a deep yellow color and she was dehydrated. After explaining that I could start an IV to rehydrate her and get her to a hospital three hours away, Madeline said she would be okay; she would just increase her fluid intake and try to get over this bug. Because this would be a refusal of treatment against medical advice (AMA), I had to make sure Madeline was competent to refuse care, was not under the influence of alcohol or drugs, and knew the possible consequences of refusal. After this was all done, she signed the waiver and off I went.

We had several service calls and separated-party calls until just before 8:00 p.m. I was called to respond to the Visitor Center (VC) lobby for a report of a 65-year-old female who had heart palpitations and felt weak. Luckily, I had just pulled into the VC parking lot and was in the lobby within one minute. Betty was from southern California and the medical history she brought along included mitral valve prolapse in her heart and paroxysmal supraventricular tachycardia (PSVT). PSVT is when the upper part of the heart starts to beat very quickly and the lower part tries its darnedest to keep up, sometimes reaching pulse rates of 240 to 270 a minute! At this rate, there is very little time for blood to enter the upper part of the heart to be pushed into the lower part of the heart to go to the lungs and the body. The person gets weak and shaky, and it can become very serious. The answer is to stop the circle (or circus) rhythm so the heart can slow down to its normal 60 - 80 beats per minute. The first thing to try is the body's own brake system for the heart, the vagus nerve. The vagus is the tenth cranial nerve and runs down from the brain along the trachea next to the carotid artery. It goes to the heart, the gut and ultimately to the rectum. The more the vagus nerve fires, the slower the heart goes. It's a good check-and-balance for the heart, unless there is a pathology that makes it not very helpful. I have responded to people with weak hearts who have sat on the toilet to have a bowel movement. They sometimes bore down so hard to defecate that they stimulated their vagus nerve enough to stop their heart! We called these commode codes and they were not a pretty sight. If we could get there fast enough to administer the drug atropine, which inhibits the effects of the vagus nerve, perhaps the heart could start to beat on its own.

In the case of PSVT, if we could stimulate the vagus nerve, it might be able to slow the heart from a 240 pulse to a more normal rate. In the past we've put our fingers over the carotid artery on one side of the neck and have pushed in a small circle to stimulate the adjacent vagus nerve into firing. This was always done after listening to the carotid artery with a stethoscope. Plaque build-up in the artery can often make a vortex sound called a bruit. But there is still a chance of breaking off a piece of plaque during a carotid sinus massage (CSM) and creating a possible stroke situation, as that piece of broken plaque rushes up into the brain.

So CSM is rarely performed and less risky ways of stimulating the vagus nerve are used. I often had patients put their thumbs in their mouths and blow as hard as they could. They inevitably forced their abdominal muscles to bear down on the vagus nerve in their gut and rectum. If vagal maneuvers didn't work, then a variety of drugs were available to try to slow the heart down, but then patient care became complicated and potentially dangerous.

Soon Dave, David and Linda arrived to help with Betty's care. She was really hypertensive, 200/110, and although her pulse was only 108, that 108 was irregular. Betty had moist skin and an anxious look on her face. You could sometimes tell when a patient was very afraid just by how they looked at you. We started her on oxygen and put her on the gurney. I placed the EKG pads on her chest, discreetly under her button-down shirt so as not to expose her to the world. I saw an underlying normal sinus rhythm on the monitor with premature atrial contractions at about eight per minute. I thought her heart was threatening to go into PSVT, but wasn't there yet.

It was dark outside and when we learned Flight For Life was on another call in Pahrump, Nevada, so we called for a fixed-wing to take Betty to the hospital. I talked to the Base Station Physician and he ordered morphine for Betty. It did seem to calm her, but her anxiety and irregular heartbeat continued. It also brought her blood pressure down, to 190/80. Betty was waiting in an ambulance when the airplane landed at the airstrip just over a mile away. We turned her over to the medical crew on board. We drove back to the VC before the fixed-wing took off to restock. As I got out of the ambulance, I pulled down the heart monitor/defibrillator and realized the EKG leads were missing. I called the flight crew on the radio and, sure enough, they were still on Betty. They would wait for someone to dash back over and pick them up. So as the ambulance drove back to the airstrip, I stood on the sidewalk of the VC in the dark, with the leadless LifePak 5 hanging from my hand. Suddenly, a naturalist came running out of the VC and said to me, "Someone just called on the phone to say a man has collapsed on stage at the Fiddler's Contest."

I looked south to Furnace Creek Ranch, a doughnut hole of private land in the National Park area, and began to run. Within 150 feet I was outside of my jurisdiction and on private land in Inyo County. We had a mutual aid agreement: we assisted the Deputy Sheriff and he assisted us. But generally, we needed to be asked to respond; we didn't routinely patrol the area. It was dark as I pulled out my radio and asked the ambulance to return Code 3 from the airport to the stage area. Through a small opening in the bushes, I was confronted with a wall of folding chairs and people, standing and sitting but not moving, all staring at the stage. I continued my run, knowing close to 1,500 people were present in the audience. Like a training obstacle course, I worked my way to the stage and jumped from the dark, lower audience area to the brilliantly lit stage. It was a large platform that could easily hold 20 to 30 people. In the middle, below the microphone stand near a railing, lay a 66-year-old male who looked to me like he was dead. Despite bystanders doing pretty good CPR, Weston was cyanotic (blue).

I knelt down next to him and ripped open his shirt. I asked for CPR to stop as I did a look, listen and feel. No pulse, no respirations. I pulled the heart monitor/defibrillator to the side and without EKG leads, did a quick look with the paddles; it was V Fib. I charged the defibrillator, gelled the paddles and after charging and calling clear, defibrillated him. After the contraction of his chest, I continued to hold the paddles to his torso and looked over to see asystole. Damn. I still didn't have my EKG leads and I was not in a position to defibrillate, so I called out loudly for tape. Within seconds I had duct tape and I securely taped the paddles to Weston's chest to continue to receive a rhythm readout from the monitor. CPR was again begun with the paddles moving up and down with each compression. Dave and Don arrived with EMS equipment and my medical bag and I went to work. I placed an OPA and had Dave start bagging 100% oxygen into Weston's lungs with the bag-valve mask. After a few breaths, I took my place at the top of Weston's head. With the laryngoscope in my left hand and an 8mm endotracheal tube (ET) in my right, I placed the tip of the tube through the vocal cords into his trachea, pulled out the stylet that gave the tube stiffness, and inflated the balloon at the end of the tube to prevent emesis or vomit from going into his lungs. I asked Don, the local Deputy Sheriff, for some tape and I turned around to see him pull about three feet of tape from a medical tape roll. It made me smile briefly and realize that I had to be more specific in my requests. As I used part of the wealth of tape to secure the ET tube in place, I looked around at the sea of people in the audience. No one seemed to be leaving; if anything, it looked like even more people were standing in the back of the sea of folded chairs, their occupants silently watching the drama unfolding before them.

Only minutes had elapsed, and Randy had an IV set ready to go. But there were no veins visible in either of Weston's arms. So, in the bright light of the stage, I placed a finger at the base of his neck on the right side, away from the carotid artery. Sure enough, a vein began to fill with blood that was passively draining the brain and could not return to the heart because of my finger pressure. It was an external jugular vein. With a syringe attached to a catheter, I asked someone else to occlude the vein as I carefully slid the needle in the catheter into the vein, pulling back on the syringe to confirm when I was in. I certainly wanted to be careful here. There were a lot of anatomical structures that could be accidentally pierced here, from arteries to trachea to lung. But within seconds I was in and I taped the IV to the right side of the jaw and neck and had someone hold it high into the air.

As I looked back at the monitor, I was surprised to see something new. Perhaps it was the 100% oxygen or excellent CPR, but when I asked them to stop CPR, I no longer saw a flat line, but a continuous set of jagged up and down peaks ... V Fib. Happy Days!

I immediately charged and defibrillated, still V Fib. I did this three times, increasing the joules or energy output each time, but with each defibrillation I only saw V Fib. So now I started the drugs, the ACLS drugs. ACLS is taught throughout the world, and is a standard set of protocols for treating full arrests. I pushed the epinephrine (epi), circulated it, and then defibrillated. More epi, another shock, and again Weston's heart entered asystole. I pushed the atropine, and within seconds I got V Fib again. I defibrillated and now I saw a recognizable and coherent set of EKG patterns. The complexes showing on the monitor were only every now and then, but the heart was trying. However, there was no pulse corresponding to the electrical discharges on the monitor. The electrical system and heart muscle were not communicating. We call this electrical-mechanical disassociation.

It had been about a half hour since my arrival and the ambulance was parked just out of sight on the road to the airport about 30 feet away. The EKG leads had returned earlier and we had placed those on Weston's chest. Once again the rhythm changed to asystole. Damn. We continued with the medications, atropine, bicarb, epi, but there was no change. I inched toward the feet of the patient and, as CPR continued, placed a call to the Base Station Physician. The asystole had lasted almost 20 minutes. There was no sign of life. The doctor said I could call the code. I thanked him and, with the team of rescuers around me continuing CPR, bagging the patient with oxygen and holding the IV high in the air, I whispered to them that I was going to call the code per doctor's orders ... but not here on stage. I learned my lesson last year at Stovepipe Wells. I didn't want the onlookers to see Weston die on stage. Who knew what hidden ailments among the 1,500 onlookers might be triggered under that stress?

So we began the short charade. We placed Weston on a backboard and strapped him down. We continued the CPR and bagging. As a unit, we lifted him up and off the back of the high stage to a group of waiting hands who placed him on the gurney. We loaded the gurney in the ambulance, turned on the lights and drove slowly toward the airport. At the turnaround, I called the code. The back of the ambulance opened and Don stuck his head in. I was alone with Weston, but Don told me he had Weston's wife Lois outside. I jumped out into the lights that had come on when the back door was opened and saw a small woman, almost 70 years old. I saw that she knew and took her in my arms for a big hug and told her how sorry we were; that we had tried everything. She cried and said she knew; she had seen our long and drawn-out efforts. She just wanted to say goodbye to him. I said of course, but that I could not leave her alone with him. She understood and I helped her up into the ambulance. As soon as she saw his lifeless body, she wailed and fell across him, sobbing and calling him, "Baby, oh my baby." It struck me as odd to hear such terms of endearment from an older woman, but it also told me the years of affection that had built up between them and taught me that no matter how old you are, someone can still be your "baby." After her time with Weston, she was lowered into the waiting arms of many friends. I learned from Don that Weston's only medical history was of arthritis and hypertension.

We received permission from the coroner to move the body, and the ambulance went to Cow Creek, the administrative and work area for the National Park Service, several miles north of Furnace Creek. As I watched the ambulance drive away, I stood next to Don in the dark. I guess it must have been to relieve the tension, and humor is often a way EMS personnel survive stressful situations. I turned to Don and said, "You know, last year I ran a code on stage at Stovepipe Wells in front of 400 people. This year I ran a code on stage at Furnace Creek in front of 1,500 people. I think my next code should be on stage at Carnegie Hall!"

CUFFS

Half of the year at Grand Canyon I worked the dayshift. The other six months I worked the nightshift. Nightshift is an entirely different world. It is less oriented toward tourist needs and more oriented to the dark side of many residents. The holidays were the worst. People stuck indoors with the cold weather, lost their temper more, drank more and fought more. Despondency, depression and suicidal thoughts made this an unhappy time for many, and it took its toll on us Rangers, also.

We were stretched thin one cold fall night when, close to midnight, I received a call to a fight at one of the local housing units. My backup was busy on another call so I went directly, intending to just listen in and wait. I received a further report of injuries and an unconscious person in the TV room. I pulled up and approached with care. I peered into the window and saw an unconscious man on the couch, but no one else.

I carefully entered the room and saw a second man sitting upright in a chair just below the window I had looked in, so was unable to see him initially. He appeared to be asleep and was snoring loudly. I carefully approached the man on the couch. He had bloodied knuckles and a bruise on his face. As I got closer, I could smell the odor of digested alcohol. His breathing was regular and his color good. I called this information in to Dispatch who informed me that my backup was still delayed. I quietly and carefully approached the man in the chair who was also bruised. Unlike the man on the couch, I could not easily see his hands to ascertain if they were empty. As I leaned over to the left to see his right hand, he started and woke up. I stepped back and told him to show me his hands. He, too, was inebriated and it took several commands before he complied. He started to get up and I told him to stay put as he approached me with open and empty hands.

I told him to turn around and put his hands behind his back and he did so. I was surprised at his easy compliance as I took his two thumbs into my left fist and began a quick pat down search. He was a big guy, well over six feet tall and two hundred plus pounds. However, he was docile and compliant and I chose not to say anything to arouse him until I completed my "Terry" search. "Terry" is from case law and allows an officer to search only for weapons as a safety precaution during an investigation. As I worked my way down his right pant leg, I noted he had boots on under his denim jeans. As I reached to the inside of his leg, I felt the hilt of a very large knife, the hilt easily two inches wide and six inches long under his pants and inside his boot. As soon as I touched it, the suspect alerted and realized I had found his concealed weapon. He pulled to release his thumbs from my grip as he began to bend over for the knife.

I reacted quickly, more from an instinct for survival than anything else. My grip was weakening on his thumbs so I let go suddenly and his hands sprang out to his sides. I quickly grabbed the bottom of his pants by the cuffs and pulled up with all my might. He was airborne. With his pant cuffs in my hands he careened over onto his chest and face and landed on the carpeted floor with a loud "thunk." I was quickly on him, placed him in an arm lock and pulled out my handcuffs as I held his torso down with a knee to his shoulder and back. With one click I got my handcuffs on him and commanded him to bring his other arm to his back. He did and I clicked it into the cuffs, double locking and checking for tightness. I completed my "Terry" search and pulled out an unsheathed hunting knife with an eight-inch blade. I ordered him not to move while I got off the floor and radioed my situation, and that I needed backup now, with one in custody. As I kept an eye on my two suspects, I soon heard the seesaw of complementary snores from the two drunks who both eventually "went south" to jail. ❏

T-Bone

I t's really important to have continuing education (CE) to stay
current in all facets of our job. We had structural fire, law
enforcement, search and rescue and emergency medical services (EMS) CE all the time, in addition to the mandatory sessions
every year.

Cow Creek was about thirty miles from my assigned station
at Stovepipe Wells. It was the location for the ambulance and fire
engines for that region of the park and the best place to gather
for CE so that the distractions of headquarters were minimized.
On this Saturday in November, one of our Base Station
Physicians had traveled to the valley to conduct our CE and
then enjoy a weekend of camping with his family. Our EMS
coordinator was also named Nancy. She set up the training, made
sure folks knew about it and kept records of attendance. We had
a good turnout that day with numerous advanced life support
providers. By the end of training, it was almost 5:00 p.m. and the
sun had dropped over the Panamint Mountains. I got into my
patrol car and started the drive north to Stovepipe Wells.

At about 5:10 p.m., I was approaching the curve to go east toward the sand dunes and home when I saw a plume of dirt in the distance to the north. I thought it was peculiar as it didn't have the wispiness of a dust devil; it went high into the air like a linear mushroom cloud. While I was contemplating this odd sight, I noted in my rearview mirror a blue sedan approach from behind and then pass me at a very high rate of speed. I was in a marked patrol car and going the speed limit. "These guys are just asking to be stopped," I thought to myself, and obliged them.

I turned on my overhead lights and activated my siren as we headed west on the road to Stovepipe. Here the road had no shoulder and there was nowhere to really pull off. Traffic was light, and I pulled about twenty feet behind the sedan that had immediately complied to my lights and sirens. I called the rear plate in to Dispatch and then cautiously approached the vehicle. From the left rear door I could see two men with dark hair in the front seat. I could see their hands, and they were empty. I called to the driver and asked him to turn the car off. He immediately complied. "This is going very smoothly," I thought. I moved up a little more and asked for the operator's driver's license. He gave me his Argentina passport and said his license was in the trunk. He moved as if to open the door and I told him to stop and keep his hands where I could see them. I asked him why he was going so fast and what possessed him to pass a police officer?

Before he could answer, I heard behind me the sound of a car accelerating at a high rate of speed. I stepped back behind the Argentine car as I watched a gray sedan come to a literal screeching halt behind my patrol car. Two persons burst from the car and ran toward me. My hand slipped to my sidearm as the possibilities flashed through my head. Was this a set up? As they came closer, I distinguished a man and a woman yelling.

"An accident, a terrible car accident!" they yelled. They stopped near me to say there had been an accident with hurt people everywhere and I had to help them. They said it was at the intersection of the Beatty Road and the Scottys Castle Road – a place we called the Mushroom, because of the shape of the information kiosk there.

The plume of dirt, I thought to myself. That dirt must have been the collision. But the hills had blocked my view of the actual roadway and the crash. It was about two miles from my current location.

I told the reporting persons I'd be right there, went up to the Argentine car, tossed the passport in and said, "Slow down!" as I jogged back to my patrol car. I turned around in the road and sped to the left-turn lane to go north to the Mushroom. I got on the radio and called for "all available personnel" to respond with the little information I knew. As I came over the rise I saw the accident scene to the left of the roadway.

A large red van traveling north had been t-boned – hit right in the side – by a gray sedan that had come downhill from the east at an extremely high rate of speed. The van had been hit so hard that in addition to rolling sideways, it had gone nose over rear bumper a few times, landing in the desert off the roadway. It lay covered in dust. The sedan rested on its roof about 150 feet farther into the desert. After coming to a halt, I pulled off my clip-on tie, threw my felt flat hat on the passenger's seat and opened my car door. I rolled up my sleeves and put on medical gloves as I surveyed the scene before me. I walked to my trunk and pulled out my medical bag. The reporting party couple had followed me back and asked if they could help. A man on a bicycle was already on scene and was next to the van. I asked the couple to wait, that I would need them, but just to stand by. I walked up to the van and saw a woman covered by so much settling dust that when she opened her eyes, it startled me. The bicyclist had helped her from the van and had seated her on the ground with her back against the roof since the van had settled on its side.

"Are you alright?" I quickly asked the woman.

"I think so," was her immediate reply.

She may have been hurt, but she had an airway and was breathing, and she was with the program enough to comprehend and answer my question.

"Can you stay with her?" I asked the bicyclist. He said yes, and I asked him not to move her any further, that I would be right back. I was in full triage mode. Triage is a word we use in medicine that helps us in mass casualty situations. Mass casualties don't have to be scores of people, just more than the rescuers can handle. At this moment, with one of me and who knew how many more injured, this was a mass casualty situation and my first priority was to locate all of the victims, to briefly stabilize any where a quick maneuver might open an airway, and to prioritize order of care and evacuation for responding units.

I jogged into the desert. I could still see in the dusk of the day, but the light wouldn't last more than thirty more minutes. I went toward the car and noticed a man just a few feet away. He had obviously been ejected from the car and the car must have rolled over him as it continued into the desert. He looked to be in his late twenties and about 160 pounds. He was lying on his back and there were $20 dollar bills in the bushes and on the ground around him. He was also cyanotic. He had sustained a crushing injury to his head. There was brain matter oozing out from his ears where his head had been compressed from front to back. There was also considerable blood loss from the crushed bones and tissue. The blood surrounded his head and was slowly seeping into the dry desert floor. He was dead and there was nothing I could do for him. In the world of triage he was last, and I could spend no more time with him. I had a roll of tape with me and wrote the time and my initials on the tape then peeled off a length the width of his head. I tore it off and placed it over his eyes. His eyes had been open and his pupils were fixed and dilated. I guess I just felt a need to close his eyes and the tape served that purpose.

My next stop was the car. It was on its roof and inside was a man on his hands and knees. I got down to look inside and the man was yelling at the top of his lungs all of the expletives and swear words I had ever heard, plus some new ones. There was the odor of alcohol coming from the car and as I looked closer, I saw cans of beer in and around the accident scene, some intact, some opened, some smashed. In fact, the more I looked the more cans I saw. It alarmed me because I guessed there had to be a lot of people around to drink that much beer. I called to the man in the car, who I later learned was 24 years old. He was yelling as if he were angry. He kept yelling; I called louder but he just kept on with his wild rantings. It was quickly apparent that he was altered, not with the program. However, that he was awake and yelling indicated that he had an airway, and that allowed me to continue on with my triage. I called over to the couple on the roadway and asked one to come out to the car. I asked this Good Samaritan, a man in his thirties, to just keep talking to the guy in the car. I told him that he should not be offended by the patient, as he had no clue what he was saying. I asked the bystander to call me if there were any changes.

I then continued in my search, looking for divots in the ground, dust on bushes and any other signs of a patient or body. About 20 feet from the car my diligence paid off when I found a 37-year-old male face down in the desert. He was unconscious and unresponsive. His ears, nose, mouth, and a variety of lacerations all spilled blood onto the ground. He was about 170 pounds and I could not feel a radial pulse in his wrist. His breathing was labored at about eight per minute and I placed my stethoscope on his back and heard his heart beat at about 120. I called to the other bystander and asked her to come to this patient. I asked her merely to stay by his side until I made sure all of the patients were accounted for, that right now, there was little more to do. I went further out into the desert until I was sure there was no one else. In a large spiral, I worked my way back to the car to be sure I hadn't missed anyone. I called an update to the responding units.

"There is one DOA (dead on arrival), one unconscious and unresponsive, one conscious but altered, and one conscious and alert," I reported.

I still needed the world to arrive but it would take a while. I looked toward Stovepipe Wells Village and in the darkening twilight saw the red, blue and amber lights of the Stovepipe Wells ambulance headed my way. I was listening to radio traffic as I heard the Furnace Creek ambulance and the fire engine respond. I radioed Dispatch with my request for a medical helicopter.

I then started round two. I went back to the lady who was sitting next to the van. The bicyclist was quietly talking to her and she seemed okay but stunned. I hunched down to get eye-to-eye contact with her and took her wrist to feel a pulse. When she looked at me she said, "Nancy," and I was stunned to recognize her as a friend and fellow park employee.

"Esy!" I exclaimed. "Are you okay? What happened?"

Esy said her hips, legs and hands hurt. She said she was headed home north, to Scottys Castle when, out of nowhere, this car t-boned her and sent her end over end, whirling around into the desert. Luckily she had her seatbelt on but the lap belt portion had left substantial bruises and abrasions on her upper thighs. Her hands hurt from gripping the steering wheel so hard. She said a toolbox flew right by her head and she was lucky it didn't hit her. Her left hand had a laceration and she could hardly grip anything, her palms were so sore. But she was alert and in good health. I told her to hang in there and that I would be back. I left her with the bicyclist and continued on my rounds.

I next went to the overturned car and the man inside was less vocal but what he said was chilling.

"I can't breathe!" he exclaimed, and continued to beat on the down-turned roof of the car while on his hands and knees. I called to him to crawl to me, that I would help him. He was oblivious to my voice and never acknowledged he could hear me. After several attempts to get him to come to me, I asked the earnest bystander to keep calling to him and to try to get him to crawl out of the crashed sedan. I later learned the patient's name was Michael.

I had been carrying an oxygen tank with me on this second round and when I got to the unconscious victim, I again checked his vital signs. He was still bleeding and breathing with difficulty. I turned on the oxygen and placed the mask next to his face that was turned to the side in the sand. I didn't want to move him without help. I was sure he had at least a broken neck in addition to his severe head injuries. I later learned his name was Michael also. I called a patient update to the responding units and the order of triage priorities. I was told that a medical helicopter was inbound to our location.

Finally, the Stovepipe Wells ambulance arrived with Rangers Russ and Roger. I went back to the roadway and filled them in on the 901 (a dead body) and the triage order of care. Roger went out to unconscious Michael in the sand, and Russ to yelling Michael (Mike) in the car. I went with Russ and by this time Mike was outside of the car. The bystander said he just started to crawl out of the car away from his voice, but then collapsed on the sand adjacent to the vehicle. We were administering oxygen when the cavalry arrived from Furnace Creek. Patrol cars, an ambulance, the fire engine and crew all arrived in succession. The ambulances, one from Stovepipe Wells and one from Furnace Creek, were parked back door to back door on the roadway.

I took Paramedic Nancy to Mike, who had crawled outside of the car. Together with Russ we gently rolled him onto his back as he continued to gasp, despite the high-flow oxygen by nonrebreather mask that was being administered. A quick set of vital signs showed he was tachycardic but had an okay blood pressure. However, his lung sounds were severely diminished on both sides and there was the beginning of a strange phenomenon. The skin at his neck, from his clavicles (collarbones) to his chin, was mottled and purple. The skin itself had a bumpy texture, like rice krispies were just underneath. These formations crackled under the touch of our fingers. Nancy set up and began an IV wide open with a 16-gauge catheter in his right arm. After we put out heads together, we were sure he had a tension pneumothorax. I cleansed the right side of his chest and placed my finger on the jugular notch at the top of his sternum. I let my finger slide to the right side of his chest until I was about midway across then dropped down to the second intercostal space. Placing a 14-gauge catheter on the top of the rib below, I pushed straight to his back and entered his chest cavity. I had to be careful not to hit the bottom of the rib above. There are blood vessels and nerve bundles that could be pierced if the needle thoracotomy was done incorrectly. I pulled out the needle and a whoosh of air came through the catheter. Nancy and I turned to each other and smiled with relief; our diagnosis had been correct. As more help arrived, Mike was placed securely on a backboard with full spinal precautions. He was put in the ambulance facing north on the roadway, waiting for the medical helicopter.

I turned my attention to the Michael who had been unconscious from the start. We were still short of help so I quickly started two 14-gauge IVs in each of his arms as he lay prone on the desert. An EMT held his head in place and the oxygen flowed from a non-rebreather mask. Finally, and with lots of help, we carefully turned him onto his back onto a backboard with full spinal precautions and carried him to the second ambulance on the road, facing south. Joe jumped in with the patient to manage the airway. It was a mess, with blood from his nose, mouth and ears. Suctioning was a priority so we could place a pharyngeal tracheal lumen (PTL) airway into his battered throat. His blood pressure had been 58/0 with a pulse of 120; but now we could not record a blood pressure and barely felt a pulse. He had to have internal bleeding and I started a third IV in his external jugular vein while the medical antishock trousers (MAST) were placed on the patient. That was a time when we still had it in our protocol to use MAST for these situations. By this time, a bag-valve mask (BVM) had been added to the PTL and we were breathing for the patient. I placed the EKG pads on his chest and the heart monitor showed a wiry pattern with occasional beats.

In the meantime, Greg had taken over Esy's care and she had been packaged onto a backboard to protect any spinal injuries and placed on oxygen. She was given blankets and, with no room in the ambulances, waited under the bright lights of the fire engine until ground transport could take her to the hospital in Las Vegas.

I received a message to go to the other ambulance to talk to Nancy. As I left Michael and scooted into the back of the other ambulance, I was stopped in my tracks at the sight of Mike. He was quite literally the "Michelin Man." The skin from his eyebrows to his knees was inflated to huge proportions. There was a tear somewhere in his respiratory system that was escaping to the layer beneath his skin, and with every breath he took, air was leaking. He was being skinned alive with every breath. It's called subcutaneous (SQ) emphysema and I had never seen it so dramatically presented. Nancy had her hands full. With his increased shortness of breath, she had done a second needle thoracostomy on Mike's chest with air return. But then he stopped breathing all together and she had placed a PTL and now his every breath came courtesy of whoever was squeezing the BVM. But with every squeeze, he got bigger and bigger. Without the BVM, he would die within minutes of lack of oxygen. All of his clothes had been cut off per standard protocol to check for further injuries and Nancy prepared to start a second IV. We pulled the sheet down and, as we did so, his genitals were exposed. We both paused in astonishment at their incredible size. The SQ emphysema had not spared these appendages. His scrotum was huge, easily the size of a football. His penis was equally large, beyond the largest cucumber I have ever seen. We were mesmerized for a brief moment, then covered him up and went to work.

Within a few minutes, Mike's carotid pulse slipped away. I jumped out of the ambulance to get the heart monitor/defibrillator (M/D) that was on Michael. We had only one M/D in Death Valley in those days, and I unplugged it from Michael and brought it back to Mike. In the interim, CPR had begun and there was an EMT working the BVM and one doing chest compressions. I looked at the monitor and Nancy hooked Mike up as I called out "V Fib." She took the paddles and began the Advanced Cardiac Life Support (ACLS) Protocols. She defibrillated him; I pushed drugs, epinephrine, lidocaine and more. She continued to defibrillate him until she received asystole ... flatline. More drugs, more CPR. I was then asked to report to the other ambulance ... CPR had just begun on Michael.

I grabbed our one M/D and hopped from the back of one ambulance into the other. We hooked him up and he too had V Fib. I shocked him three times but he persisted in his V Fib as we began the ACLS protocols on him. As I was pushing epinephrine down the IV line, I could hear the whirr of the medical helicopter above us. Flight Nurse Donna came to my door and I quickly filled her in on my patient. Then she went to Nancy's ambulance and quickly returned. They were going to call the code on Mike and take Michael to Las Vegas. I looked at her skeptically. We briefly discussed it. Neither patient was likely to survive, but at least Michael wasn't flatline yet. As Donna entered with her heart M/D, I detached mine and jumped out of Michael's ambulance and into Mike's ambulance. We hooked Mike back up and he was still in asystole. Nancy called on the radio to the Base Station Physician. No more drugs were being pushed, but the BVM was still pushing oxygen into and out of the patient as CPR compressions continued. Finally, Nancy got the word to call the code and pronounced Mike dead at 6:04 p.m.

I jumped out of the ambulance as Nancy sat on the bench seat. They were loading Michael into the helicopter. There was blood oozing profusely from his wounds and it was very pink with the IV fluids that had been added. I had put three liters into him and Donna had replaced my bags with three more. She appealed for a small person to go along to do chest compressions. Fire Chief Kent pointed to Juan. Juan pulled off his turnout coat and jumped into the helicopter. I could see him hunched over Michael doing compressions as the helicopter took off into the night sky.

When I returned to Mike's ambulance, the word had gotten out about the SQ emphysema. Those who had never seen it before came and looked at the grotesque size the skin had stretched to. It looked as if Mike might explode at any second. After most had left, Joe came over and took one look at the huge proportions of the blown-up genitals and asked aloud, "Does he have a donor card?"

We had a lot of cleanup to do and the light from the fire engine lit the scene. One Ranger stood vigil next to the first deceased in the sand, waiting for the coroner to call to give permission to move the body. Medical supplies and oxygen tanks were gathered up. One person walked over with a wallet and opened it. There were hundreds and fifties almost one-half inch thick, easily over a thousand dollars. It had been payday at the mines in Beatty, Nevada. But it was a short celebration for those who drink and drive.

I then heard, "Irish, hey Irish!" I turned to see Kent call me from the roadway. I walked over as he told me there had been an "incident" with the medical helicopter with Donna, Juan and the patient. Others heard and rushed over. He quickly related that as the helicopter had been coming in to land, it was over the roof of the hospital when it suddenly caught fire! It seemed all of those leaking fluids had drained into the helicopter's wiring system in the belly and shorted something out. They were able to land and get out safely, but it was a scare. We also learned that Michael had never converted his heart to a workable rhythm and had been declared dead at the hospital. We all deflated at the news, but then reflected on Juan's near miss. At least he had his turnout pants on. We later learned that Mike had transected his trachea, an injury so severe that it was really quite remarkable that he lived as long as he did. We felt bad for the three men who died. We later learned they were miners. But we felt good that every-thing possible had been done to save them. We later heard that Esy had arrived safely to the hospital in the ground ambulance and was sore but okay. Thank goodness she was wearing her seat-belt.

GUN

David was a big guy – a really big guy; easily twice my size. You wouldn't think he would be very fast, given his size, but one night I found out just how fast he could be. We had responded in separate vehicles to a report of a disturbance at the Victor Hall Annex in Grand Canyon. It's an all-male dormitory for the employees of the concessionaire. David was upstairs at the far end of the hall from me, interviewing a suspect. I was outside, downstairs, approaching a lone female occupant in the front passenger seat of a parked sedan. She cracked the door and, as I started to ask her name and her business, I spotted a .45 caliber semiautomatic pistol wedged to her left between her seat and the console. I pulled the door open, grabbed both of her hands and pulled her from the vehicle onto the ground. I commanded she lie face down as I drew my pistol and simultaneously pulled my radio from my belt. I said only one word over the radio, "Gun," and then turned my attention back to the female suspect who was inebriated and having a hard time complying with my commands. Within seconds I heard a thunderous pounding as David raced down the hallway and two flights of stairs to back me up with his gun drawn. He was there in seconds. I was blown away with the speed and intensity of his response, and very grateful for the backup. David and I worked together a lot and he never ceased to amaze me. This was one of those moments. ❏

Heat and Lightning

■ Grand Canyon, Arizona

They say only fools and Rangers hike in the canyon in the summer time. It is so very hot and taxing. People lose their appetite and don't eat enough to continue. They don't drink enough water. Psychologically, they cannot go back up when they look at the 5,000 feet of canyon they have to climb after the pretty easy descent. Whatever the reason, summer hikers provide job security for Rescue Rangers. For pleasure, the best times to enter the canyon are March and November. As a rule of thumb, the temperature in Phoenix, Arizona, is the same temperature in the shade at Phantom Ranch at the bottom of the Bright Angel and Kaibab Trails. But these are shade temperatures. It can be 112 degrees Fahrenheit at Phantom in the shade and perhaps 125 to 140 degrees in the direct sun. You can lose one to three liters of water per hour hiking in those conditions. Fluid replacement is vital and carrying a gallon of water with you is not enough on most days in the summer.

From the village area on the south rim of the canyon, there is a delightful 30-mile drive to Desert View called East Rim Drive.

It has numerous overlooks and allows a true change of scenery from one point to the next. Some of the overlooks are trailheads into the canyon. Grandview, Hance and New Hance are rough trails but doable. They are certainly not as frequently traveled as the village trails. There is no water available and hikers must be experienced and resourceful to tackle these trails any time of the year, let alone during the summer.

For the 4th of July, Todd traveled from Indiana to join his friend Brandon, from Albuquerque, for a round of golf in Flagstaff. At 7,000 feet, it was warm but pleasant, and the two friends decided they would drive to the Grand Canyon the next day. It was only a ninety-minute drive and the view was spectacular. They continued their drive along the East Rim and stopped at Grandview Overlook. There, the trail to Horseshoe Mesa was an open invitation, and the two friends decided to go for a short walk down the Grandview Trail. It was steep but deceptively easy. Each carried a 12-ounce bottle of sports drink. After three miles, they were out of fluids. Todd decided he would continue down to the Colorado River. He estimated that it couldn't be too far away and would catch a ride with a boat crew to Phantom Ranch to the west. Brandon wasn't keen about the idea. He thought going back up the three miles of trail was safer. The choice became easier when they became separated. Todd went off trail to climb a ridge to locate access to the river. Brandon lost sight of him and, after a lengthy wait, hiked the long trail back to the trailhead.

The canyon has a history of being deceptive. When the conquistadors of the Coronado expedition, under the supervision of Don Pedro de Tovar, arrived at the south rim of the canyon in 1540, they thought the river was a short distance away. They scrambled down to find a way to the river for a resupply of water. They soon realized that the distances were not what they seemed. Rocks they thought were the size of loaves of bread ended up being taller than church steeples in Seville. They scrambled back up to the south rim, never reaching the river.

Brandon made it to the Grandview overlook and thirstily drank from water back at the car. He waited there for Todd's return, ultimately spending the night in the car. The next day at 3:30 p.m., with canyon shade temperatures at 114 degrees, Brandon finally alerted the Rangers that his good friend was missing. A search was immediately begun, spearheaded by a reconnaissance flight over the area where Todd was last seen. At 1,300 feet above the Tonto Platform the helicopter spotters thought they saw something in Cottonwood Drainage. In a narrow crack, a figure was spotted laying still on a rock. It was about a mile from the river, in an area of steep cliffs and dry falls. It was fifty feet from the top of the crevice to the rock below, and no place for the helicopter to land. When the helicopter landed several miles away, Ranger Chuck hiked into the crevice where the 26-year-old Todd lay injured. Chuck, an experience I-EMT, made the hike in less than 45 minutes, climbing down to the patient and arriving by 5:00 p.m. Ranger Matt and Volunteer in the Park (VIP) Tim soon followed with additional gear. Darkness was falling when the helicopter placed Rangers Nick and Tammy on the western access point and me on the east. Nick and Tammy began working their way down to the patient. The rescuers in the crevice could not communicate directly with the Rangers on the rim because of the high canyon walls, so I stayed on the Tonto Platform as the radio relay. The helicopter was not allowed to fly after dark because there were no lights in the canyon; it also had to return to get ready for tomorrow's transport needs. I had my paramedic bag with personal survival equipment, two quarts of water I always carry in my bag, and an extra gallon "cubitainer" of water to get me through the night.

Another human radio relay, Mike, was at Grandview Point near the trailhead. He would relay all of my information to the Incident Commander at Park Operations on the South Rim. Chuck called up a patient assessment for me to relay to Mike, and then to the Base Station Physician at Flagstaff Medical Center. It was apparent to Chuck that Todd had fallen almost fifty feet onto a slab of rock. He was in an altered state, not answering questions appropriately; his skin was hot and dry to the touch and ashen in color. His eyes were glassy and his mouth was dry. He complained of being dizzy and spoke in only two-to three-word sentences. He had blood on his scalp and blood coming from his nose and mouth. Chuck heard diminished lung sounds on one side. His oral temperature was 104 degrees; he had pain in his neck, chest, abdomen and feet; and then he began to cough up blood. He had had only ingested twelve ounces of fluid in 24 hours. Chuck started an intravenous (IV) fluid drip on Todd and used his own drinking water to wet Todd to cool him out of his heat stroke. He tied a piece of webbing around Todd's pelvis to keep him from sliding down the tilted rock and hand-stabilized his head to protect his cervical spine until help came. He also gave him oxygen intermittently from his one cylinder.

Chuck and I talked sparingly to preserve radio batteries. In between these conversations, I stood up on the Tonto Platform and looked around. There was no one else for miles. I was truly alone on the nearly flat ground. A short distance from the edge of the crevice was a single rock about two feet high and two feet long – the only upward solid projection among the soft bushes and short grasses. I watched the sun set amidst the gathering storm clouds, which made for a brilliantly colored display. Lightning flashed somewhere in the distance and I could hear the distant booming of thunder.

Just after 9:30 p.m., Matt, Tim, Tammy and Nick reached Chuck and Todd. Chuck had done a brilliant job getting Todd's temperature down to 100 degrees and getting several liters of IV fluid into his system. Chuck reported to me by radio that Todd had better color and was more alert. The down side of this improved physical appearance was that the increase in consciousness made Todd more aware of his pain and thirst. They packaged Todd with spinal precautions in a full body vacuum splint and moved him to level ground. Nick took over on-scene operations and began to call up resource needs to me. I wrote them down, repeated them back to him for accuracy, and then relayed the information to Mike. As I looked up to Grandview Point, sometimes I thought I could see a flash of a light, but it was otherwise dark and overcast, with the occasional lightning flash a few miles away that lit up the night sky.

The rescuers decided that the best plan would be to travel down the drainage toward the river. They would need a sawyer team (people who work with saws) to cut vegetation and personnel to help carry Todd to safety. They had scouted the river drainage before dark and there was a sixty-foot cliff that would require a helicopter shorthaul. With Todd immobilized, a long flight of ten to fifteen minutes could have been extremely dangerous, especially since he couldn't protect his airway if he vomited. A two-minute shorthaul to a waiting helicopter on the river was much safer for him. The rescuers ordered a motorized boat to carry the patient to a safe landing zone (LZ) for the medical evacuation helicopter. (At this time, the Department of Public Safety (DPS) was becoming more involved for air transportation assistance, along with the U.S. Forest Service for manpower.)

Once I had relayed all of the information, we agreed to check in with each other every fifteen minutes. We would conserve battery power by turning off our radios. With my radio off and the apparent isolation from civilization, the scale of the huge plateau really set in. I could hear nothing but the wind and the rasp of the bushes with their small branches rubbing against each other. I heard the scurry of a mouse. It was still pretty warm and I had been rationing my water. I ate a granola bar for dinner. As I reveled in the immense wilderness, I picked up on a disturbing pattern in the sky above. The distant lightning was not so distant anymore. Strikes began to hit within two to three miles of my position. I saw the strike, started my count, one thousand one, one thousand two, etc., with every five equaling a mile. The storm was still a bit distant, but coming my way. When I checked in after midnight, I found myself talking to Tammy.

Apparently there was a situation developing that could have serious consequences. The rescuers had used most of their drinking water to cool Todd, who had stabilized. Now the rescuers were starting on that quick road to dehydration. Tammy said they would start IVs on each other to stay hydrated while Nick and Matt tried to find a way to the river in the dark to resupply. I told her I would order up extra IV fluids and associated supplies for delivery at first light, enough for all of the rescuers. She asked how I was doing. Relative to them, I was in pretty good shape. I didn't have to battle the heat they did. Down in the crevice, the heat was still radiating from the walls long after sunset, keeping it very hot there. I was on the wide open plateau with a cooling breeze approaching. My only concern was lightning. The tallest thing within a mile of my position was that small rock, so I was a bit concerned about being struck. We wished each other good luck and signed off for the next check-in. The clouds were closing in over my last glimpse of the Big Dipper. I had a small notepad and with nothing else to do; I began to write about the day before. Moths and beetles began to crowd around my headlamp, the only light for miles.

* * * *

The day was one of my very busiest. I had the shift that began at 6:00 a.m. I went down to the horse corral and fed the horses, filled their water trough, and carried forkfuls of hay to the various feeding troughs. The sun was bright, the birds were chirping; it was a great day after the 4th of July. As I walked back to my car, I checked my defensive equipment for traces of hay that can get caught here and there. I had a collapsible baton, oleoresin capsaicin (OC or pepper) spray, a 9mm Sig Sauer pistol, handcuffs, mini flashlight, latex-like gloves under my handcuffs, keys and key holder, radio and Leatherman tool. One time, another female Ranger and I were at the helibase and decided to weigh ourselves on the helibase equipment scale. We were appalled! After taking off our boots, body armor and defensive equipment, we were 23 pounds lighter.

My patrol car today was one we called the "Queen Mary," a very old and clunky barge-like Crown Victoria sedan. My newer vehicle was in the shop with transmission problems, so I was stuck with the Queen for a day ... or two. I stopped briefly at a resident's house to check on her old but sweet dog. Barb was our Dispatch supervisor, an excellent dispatcher who was out of town. Her 15-year-old Kate was fine. She often returned the favor by checking in on our 3-year-old Golden Retriever Shannon, when we were out of town, or if both Kent (my husband) and I were on a long call. I went to the Ranger Operations building and completed my last report and sent it off. I hit the roads, looking for out-of-bounds campers and anyone I might be able to help.

At 7:45 a.m., I was on East Rim Drive near Grandview when a green sedan with Colorado plates blew by me at 35 mph in a posted 25 mph zone. I radioed the plate number in to Dispatch and then made a vehicle stop. There was a young man and a woman in the vehicle, neither wearing their seatbelt. After the plate came back clear for wants and warrants, I made my approach. The woman was Talia and the driver was Christopher. I obtained their identifications and called them in to Dispatch. Within minutes, Dispatch called back with a "possible ten-thirty-five frank," on Christopher. That is radio code for a possible wanted felon. I pulled my 9mm pistol out of its holster and held it along the right side of my leg. I very calmly had them put their hands where I could always see them and explained the situation to them. I also calmly told them that if they made any sudden or threatening moves that someone could get hurt. All they had to do was sit quietly while all of this got sorted out. They replied that that was okay with them. Christopher in particular was nervous but polite, replying, "Yes, Ma'am," to my requests. Ranger John was en route to back me up. Before he arrived, Dispatch confirmed that the social security numbers didn't match up. The name was identical, but the numerical identifiers were not. I gave Christopher a verbal warning for excessive speed and no seatbelts. After they put their seatbelts on, they were free to go and did so, nice and slowly.

I headed to the helibase next. I was the assigned Flight Medic for the day and wanted to make sure all of the equipment was present and in working order. I checked the heart monitor/defibrillator, rescue equipment, drug bag, iStat machine (that can do blood chemistries in the field), suction unit, oxygen, ProPaq automatic blood pressure, and pulse and oximetry machine. I then cleared. All was in readiness.

At 10:10 a.m., backcountry Ranger Marty called in that he was responding to a report of a man having a seizure. I picked up Ranger Andy who knew I was Flight Medic that day and responded to the helibase. At the helibase I opened up my trunk, took off my uniform and replaced it with my flight suit and radio harness and shoulder holster. I grabbed my paramedic bag and went to get the rest of my Advanced Life Support (ALS) equipment. Jon was the helicopter pilot. After briefing, we took off for the Abyss and dove into the canyon. I loved that part. It's like being a soaring eagle on a dive. We skirted around to the top of the Corkscrew and I was able to pick out Marty on the trail. We landed and I put on my 40-pound paramedic pack and grabbed the heart monitor while Andy got her pack, the oxygen and drugs. We headed down the trail to Marty's location. He was with the patient, a 50-year-old man from Greece named Tery, who had a history of seizures. He had collapsed and was still very weak after having a seizure on the trail. I set all of the equipment down and began to put Tery on the heart monitor as Marty filled me in. I saw a normal sinus rhythm, which was good. Andy was busy starting a saline lock, an IV without the solution bag. She handed me a syringe with blood and I processed it in the iStat machine. In this case, the patient was a bit dehydrated, so it looked like an uncomplicated call. We slowly walked Tery to the helicopter with his saline lock in place, along with the attached heart monitor and oxygen via nasal cannula. Andy, Marty and Tery's wife stayed behind. I took Tery to the Clinic once we landed at the South Rim; he seemed to be recovering, but was still quite weak. I left to return to the helibase for the cleanup. I had to replace used supplies, refill our oxygen cylinder from the cascade system, and try to get the ubiquitous Grand Canyon red dirt off the bags and equipment.

Just as I finished the cleanup, we received a report of a 20-year-old Asian woman on the trail with chest pain and shortness of breath. In most circumstances, that is not of great concern because of her young age, but the report added that the patient had congenital heart problems. I grabbed my equipment. Jon and I again dove off the Abyss, across the formation called the Battleship, and landed at the LZ at Three-Mile-House. Starting up the trail, I carried the equipment myself because this time I was all alone. As I walked, I kept asking hikers if they knew of anyone fitting the woman's description that needed help. Several parties said there was a large group of Asians working their way up the hill but no one was asking for help. After fifteen minutes of this, I was told by radio to report back to the helicopter, that the call had been cancelled. I turned around and headed back down. It was a good workout for July. I stopped briefly and checked the emergency locker at the LZ before Jon and I took off for the helibase.

It was now 12:30 p.m., so I headed home to the duplex I share with Kent. Most people don't realize that Park Rangers pay rent and utilities to the government for housing. Because our rates are compared to Flagstaff, rents are pretty high, and so most of us have a tough time building up money to buy a house of our own somewhere.

As I changed from my flight suit to my uniform, I downed a sandwich. Then I received a report of two stolen backpacks. I was not the only Ranger on duty, but the calls were starting to build up on all of us and we had to pick up the pace to keep up. The victims were not from America. After topping out on a hike on the Bright Angel Trail, they took the free shuttle bus to Mather Campground and leaned their packs against a tree to go get lunch. On their return, their packs were gone. National Parks have changed in the last few decades and, sadly, you can't count on them being havens from lawlessness. I checked lost and found and took a report, but could not help them more than that.

Then I received a report that the Asian woman from the earlier report was being carried up the trail by her family. I headed over to the Bright Angel Trailhead, Code 3 – lights and sirens. I left my defensive gear and body armor on, put my EMS pack on my back, double-timed it down the Kolb Studios stairs and ran down the trail. Matt was just ahead of me and Chuck was coordinating the litter team and heart monitor and other equipment that would follow. Just past the Second Tunnel, about three-quarters of a mile down, Matt reported he was on scene with a stable patient and that she had no cardiac history. I arrived a moment later and helped Matt with the assessment. Her name was Wyn and she was not able to stand or walk. She was Vietnamese. I pulled her brother aside and learned that she had fainted in the past and that a doctor had told them it could be cardiac related. She was just too embarrassed to admit it to Matt.

So we put her on oxygen and the heart monitor. I started a saline lock after Matt did vital signs, including blood pressure, pulse and respirations, and she was placed on the one-wheeled litter for safe transport up the trail. The litter is a wire-mesh basket over six feet long and about two feet wide. The litter is lifted and balanced on an inflatable wheel. The patient is then pulled and pushed up the trail by a team of rescue Rangers. The haul team rotates to keep from becoming exhausted. At one such rotation stop, I re-evaluated Wyn and she looked terrible.

She was pale and out of it, with an altered level of consciousness. Her blood pressure had plummeted to 82/0 from a normal of 120/80! I quickly got out a liter of IV normal saline solution and plugged it into her saline lock and ran it wide open. We continued up the trail at a steady pace until we reached the top. Wyn's blood pressure was now 90 systolic (the upper number) and she seemed a bit more lucid. We loaded her into Medic 2, the ambulance, and took Wyn to the clinic. I had just given a report to the nurse on duty when I was told to report to the helibase. Dispatch had received a report of two severely dehydrated hikers at Tanner Wash beach. VIP Tim and I responded in the Bell Long Ranger helicopter. It was a gorgeous time to fly with the shadows forming in the canyon. When we came around the bend in the river and the Tanner area opened up in front of us, it was awe-inspiring. I have to do all of my sightseeing flying in to a call, because I am usually too busy with patient care on the way out to even look out the window. There were several beached boats and we flew over them to land above the hiker's camp. I jumped out and walked a short distance to greet a man who ran up to us. He said the hikers were in bad shape with exhaustion, tremors and cramping. He added that a commercial riverboat company with two orange boats had picked them up and were headed down stream. Now we were playing tag. As we lifted off and radioed in the results of our findings, we were told to abort the mission. This had been a frustrating day: getting called off of Wyn's call then finding her, now losing sight of these hikers at the first attempted contact. We called back the status report we had received and got permission to track down the boats. In a short distance we spotted them and landed. Tim ran over to the orange boats and then came back. The river company had successfully rehydrated the hikers who were declining any help or evacuation, so we lifted off for the helibase.

It was 7:00 p.m. when I finally walked in the door at home. Kent was home, as was Shannon and our parakeet Darby. I had peeled off my flight suit, boots and sweaty socks before the telephone rang. It was Chuck who was coordinating the rescues today. There was a possible hyponatremia patient at Phantom Ranch. Marty was on scene and there was no other advanced life support (ALS) available. Could I respond to the helibase and be prepared to spend the night? I said sure and put my flight suit back on as Kent made me a quick sandwich. I ate it while I waited for Chuck to pick me up. Marty was trying very hard to get the patient to the Delta Pad near the river at Phantom Ranch. If he couldn't, then I'd have to spend the night. There is a rule the Office of Aircraft Safety (OAS) enforces for flying at the canyon. Without a lighted and established LZ, helicopters cannot operate earlier than thirty minutes before sunrise or thirty minutes after sunset time. We call this window "pumpkin time" and we were smack in it now.

At the helibase, we rushed the equipment onto the helicopter and Jon the pilot broke some rules and flew directly over the village. I was flabbergasted. We always flew around the village to the Abyss so that we wouldn't disturb the residents or visitors. But here we were, buzzing the village and flying just above East Rim Drive west of Yaki Point and screaming into the Grand Canyon. I watched the instruments and we hit 120 knots on our dive ... great G-forces. We hurdled the black bridge that spans the Colorado River and landed at the delta in what seemed like nothing flat. Marty was at the LZ with the patient, Michael. Michael looked much older than his 39 years and had an IV established. I asked Marty who put it in. Marty said the Bureau of Land Management (BLM) VIP, Tim. Tim had been a smoke jumper out of Boise but I didn't know he could practice here. In any event, Michael was packaged and ready to go and with Marty's quick but thorough report, we were able to load Michael into the helicopter, strap him in behind the pilot and put on his helmet. I hung the IV from a ring in the back and slipped in beside him. I noted there was blood backed up in the line and it wasn't running, but that was not unusual when the IV bag is carried below the patient's heart. I shut it off until I could deal with it. Michael seemed mostly okay but was extremely fatigued. I started to take a set of vital signs as we took off within legal pumpkin time. With so much flight time in helicopters, I have learned to read lips and Michael was complaining of pain in his right arm. I checked the IV site in his right hand and it looked okay. I unzipped his flight suit, surveyed his arm and was extremely surprised to see the tourniquet still in place from the IV start. I pulled on one end to release the IV tourniquet and Michael was immediately relieved of his pain, but the IV wouldn't run, so I shut it off again.

In just a few moments, Jon turned on the intership communications and pointed out the fabulous sunset we were privileged to see. I glanced up and paused to take in the near and far clouds that picked up the pink, orange, purple and other indescribable colors. There were streaks and sunrays piercing through the monsoon clouds. I forced myself to turn my attention back to my patient. His vital signs appeared stable and I reviewed the run sheet Marty passed on to me. We landed and I slowly walked Michael to the ambulance that was waiting there for us. I placed him on the heart monitor and started a quick IV in his left arm. We arrived at the clinic and I gave report to the nurses and went back to the helibase to clean up and get everything ready for the next call. It was 9:00 p.m. by the time I got everything done and arrived back home. I telephoned Paramedic Bill, who was a summer seasonal and the emergency services field coordinator. I expressed my concern about the IV start by VIP Tim. Bill stated Tim could only start IVs when another Medic was present. Bill said he would call Tim and clarify his scope of practice. I was so exhausted by my fifteen-hour day that I crawled into bed at 9:45 p.m.

* * * *

Now, more than 24 hours later on the Tonto Platform, things had changed dramatically for me. In the survival pouch of my paramedic rescue bag, I kept plastic garbage bags. I made a hole for my head and arms and wore one like a poncho. I put my paramedic bag in another as thunder clapped and lightning flashed all around me, and the rain began to fall. I crouched down, lying on my left side with my back against that one little rock and my paramedic bag against the front of my torso. It was the best I could do. I was still the highest thing around. A few times I saw lightning, and before I could even start counting, I heard the thunder split my eardrums. It was spectacular. I remember thinking that in a different circumstance, I would really be enjoying the incredible display of nature. I tried to get even smaller. I didn't dare turn on my radio. It was in a bag all by itself on the other side of the rock. I didn't want that electronic device anywhere near me to act like a lightning rod. Tammy knew that I might not check in if the lightning got bad. I was so worried about her and the other rescuers getting heat illness from dehydration and she was worried about me getting struck by lightning.

Back in the crevice, water reserves were getting dangerously low. Matt and Nick worked their way toward the river just after 1:30 a.m. At the pour-over from the drainage to the river was a cliff that would only be safely negotiated with technical equipment in the daytime. They worked their way back up the east side of the drainage and up a cliff with a talus slope on the other side. They were successful in reaching the river, filled their water bottles and added water-purifying tablets. They then worked their way back up to the patient site.

Finally, the brunt of the storm passed and, on the next fifteen-minute interval, I checked in with Mike at Grandview and then with Tammy in the crevice. We both expressed relief at each other's survival. I relayed that it sounded like everything was in place for tomorrow's extrication. The good news about the patient was that he finally urinated. Yahoo! Hydration enough for urination was an awfully good sign. The bad news was it was the color of dark wine and tested positive for blood. There was no doubt that Todd was badly hurt with multi-system trauma. It was a miracle he survived dehydration and heat stroke, let alone the variety of fractures and internal injuries he had suffered. But morning was approaching and the extrication was about to begin.

By morning, I was wearing my orange flight suit only to my waist. The day was warm early, even at 6:00 a.m. Chuck and I talked on the radio. He sounded exhausted and they were all dehydrated. I continued to radio relay as needed. I heard a canyon wren with its downward spiraling whistle. Monsoon clouds were gathering early in the distance, with a slight breeze following the sunrise. I looked in my water bottle and there was a ball of red ants floating on the surface. Somehow they had crawled in between the threads and were clinging to each other. I tipped them out with a few precious ounces of water. There was no shade except for an occasional thin cirrus cloud just overhead that drifted in front of the sun. At 7:30 a.m., Mike relayed that the helicopter was on its way. I relayed that information to the crowd in the crevice and then strained to hear the distinctive whirr of the helicopter.

River Ranger Dave was brought in by helicopter and assembled his boat and motor on the north side of the Colorado River. There was no room on the south side of the river for an LZ. He ferried personnel, including the sawyers, across the river to the drainage. Nick and Matt had flagged the access route at first light and the crew arrived at the patient site and began cutting a swath through the wilderness to allow the patient to be carried down the drainage. Equipment carried in nets was deposited near the patient site, including water and more IV fluids, food and essentials. It was a lot of work, but by 1:00 p.m., the litter carry crew was in place. The crew consisted of six persons at a time that carried Todd down the drainage in the long basket. Carrying him by brute force over uneven terrain for a long distance was taxing, and so the team was changed out often. At the cliff face, Todd was prepared for shorthaul. He was lifted into the air at the end of a rope under the DPS helicopter to an LZ down river where the medical evacuation helicopter waited to take him to the hospital. There he was treated for a broken bone in his neck, a collapsed lung, two broken feet, a broken right elbow and internal injuries. Amazingly, Todd lived.

All of the rescuers were evacuated. It took over 55 rescue personnel to get Todd out of his predicament. It damaged natural resources of the canyon that will take years to recover. It cost close to $60,000. But it saved a life.

FIRST FLIGHT

It was May and I was a new Ranger to the Grand Canyon. I had come from Death Valley and had a lot to learn about this park's procedures, the location of things, and the names of all of my new colleagues. Once I was cleared by our Medical Control to work in Arizona, I hit the ground running. On this day just before 9:00 a.m., I was told to report to the Grand Canyon Helibase for a report of a woman with an object impaled in her eye. It certainly sounded like a bad call.

Albert was the search and rescue (SAR) coordinator and told me the location was the confluence of the Colorado River and Havasu Creek, and that there was a very narrow ledge for the helicopter to land on. He warned that it would be a dicey approach and that I could call off the landing if it seemed too hairy. Yikes! My first call as a flight medic at the Grand Canyon and I was already being told how to abort the mission! I walked over to the Bell Long Ranger Helicopter. I was very familiar with this model. A mustachioed man in a flight suit walked up with a big smile. He was obviously the pilot.

"Hi, I'm Nancy," I said, extending my right hand for a handshake. "I'm new to Grand Canyon and this is my first flight here."

"Hi, I'm Jerry and this is my first flight here, too," he said as he shook my hand in greeting.

My stunned look made him laugh as he added, "I've been flying the canyon for years and this is just my first medical flight as the backup pilot." The first-up pilot Bob was off that day.

We reviewed the call and location and, with Jerry flying the helicopter, I settled in and marveled at the incredible beauty of the Canyon from the air. I knew just how lucky I was; tourist helicopters are no longer allowed below the rim.

We flew west above the Tonto Platform and, in less than half an hour, we saw the outflow of Havasu Creek into the Colorado River far below us. The walls of the canyon were very narrow in the gorge, and the approach was beyond me. Luckily, Jerry was flying and knew just what to do. He began a slow, calculated spiral into the gorge. We made multiple circles as the walls became narrower and narrower. I could see the boats tied up near the confluence and some folks upstream of Havasu Creek waiting on the rocks. Finally, after several minutes of this precise maneuver, Jerry turned the aircraft at a right angle to the canyon wall and lowered down onto a shelf that was shorter than the ship was long. The tail of the helicopter hovered over the rapids and the whole ship was buffeted back and forth from the force of the air turbulence of the rapids. On the intership intercom, Jerry said he'd have to "stay hot" (not shut down) while I went to check on the patient. I left my medical bag in the back seat area as I opened the door to the helicopter. I worked my way between the wall and the nose of the helicopter until I could jump up toward the group of people. A young man approached me and thanked me for coming. He looked familiar, but I could not place him. I asked where the patient was and a 48-year-old woman walked up to me and said she was the patient. I looked her in both eyes and could see nothing wrong.

"I was told the patient had an impaled object in her eye," I inquired, looking beyond the lady for an explanation. Finally, the boatman of the expedition pulled me aside and explained the situation, as I looked at more people in the group.

"You can see," the boatman started, "that this is a very influential political family and there are celebrities here too." I nodded my head as I recognized many of the people he was alluding to.

"You see, when she walked down the trail from the rim two days ago, she stubbed her toes and they have hurt ever since and she wants to come out." He continued as I began to shake my head.

"What was I supposed to do?" he exclaimed.

"Not endanger a rescue crew and a helicopter for someone with stubbed toes," I answered.

It had been a truly difficult approach and landing, and I left the boatman to confer with Jerry. He was unflappable.

"Well, we're here; we might as well take her out."

I went over to the woman to escort her to the ship. She pulled up short and exclaimed that she would not leave without her husband. I was about to say something when I remembered that it would serve no purpose under the circumstances and motioned to the husband to come along. I drew the line at their baggage. I buckled them carefully into the back of the chopper and secured my own seatbelt as we took off. No spiral this time. Jerry wheeled right and headed down river in a rush, then soared up higher and higher, adding a lazy banking turn that headed us back east.

On our return to the helibase, Albert was standing by with the ambulance.

"That won't be necessary," I said. "They can go to the clinic in a patrol car."

After we arrived at the clinic, I pulled Albert aside and told him the whole story. He was livid. He said I did the right thing to bring them out, but that they were wrong to abuse the system in this manner. I was pleased to hear him relate to the powerful couple the risks we had taken to pull them out and that by using the rescue radio under false pretenses, they had broken the law. He wrote them a violation notice with a fine and left them to their own resources at the clinic. I later learned the boatman lost his job for misusing the rescue radio to broadcast a false injury.

Jerry and I still marvel at that call, even chuckle. But I always end the thought with a shake of my head and the idea that I might have lost my life for someone who had stubbed her toes. ❏

Babies

Most of the time, EMS personnel try to stabilize injured or ill patients. Sometimes, a baby delivery is added to the repertoire. I know some medics are scared to death of delivering a baby. But my training was excellent and over the years, I've delivered quite a few babies, to the point where I looked at it as an opportunity for joy. Of course, it's one thing to deliver a baby in a hospital; it's another to do so in a rural national park, hours from the nearest health care facility. Even a health care facility is not a guarantee of a routine delivery.

In my seasonal Park Ranger days during the off-season, I often worked as a city paramedic. It was a great opportunity for getting experience and fine-tuning pre-hospital skills. One winter while working as a paramedic in Fresno, California, my partner and I were taking our gurney into the children's hospital to pick up a patient for a transfer to another facility. We walked in with the gurney to the patient registration area. It had individual cubicles with doors for privacy and a large window facing the entryway. I noted an Asian man standing in front of the registrar trying to get some point across and, as I rounded the corner, I noted his wife in the corner of the cubicle sitting in a plastic chair. She was quiet but had a strained look on her face. I glanced down at her lap and noticed her skirt was hiked up to her hips and a head was protruding from between her legs!

I immediately pushed open the door to the cubicle, unwittingly smashing the husband against the far wall. I crouched down in my best shortstop position and, as I raised my arms, the rest of the baby came rushing out of the mother. I leaned forward and tried to catch the slippery newborn but it was brought up short by its neck, and its little legs came whipping around toward me. I leaned in with my whole torso and pressed the baby against the chair and mom, preventing it from any further travel. I noted with quick dismay that it was the color of a blue racquetball, and it had the umbilical cord wrapped around its little neck. That is what made it come up short and spin around as it emerged from the mom. The baby was covered in slippery amniotic fluid mixed with blood and yellow glistening tissue, part of the amniotic sac. I quickly slipped my fingers under the cord at the chin and maneuvered it from around the baby's neck. I called out to my partner to hand me the gurney sheet and get the obstetrics (OB) folks down here pronto. I opened the baby's airway very slightly and heard it take its first few breaths. Then, as it took more breaths, it began to pink up as an arm twitched and then a leg. I could feel the pulse in the umbilical cord and I put my fingers on the inside of the baby's arm to feel its brachial pulse. It was picking up steam. I dried and rubbed and stimulated the baby boy as I sat back on my knees, holding it close and literally watching it come to life in front of me. It went from purple to blue to mottled to pink and soon let out a healthy cry. I saw a neonatal incubator appear at the doorway as a nurse called out, "The baby is already here . . . it's out!"

I very reluctantly handed the baby up to the nurse, who leaned down beside me. She crouched down to be near the mom who was still in possession of the placenta and so was tied to the new baby. As I stepped outside, I saw others enter with the tools to clamp the cord, suction the baby and address the mom's needs. I saw the dad peering from behind the door with eyes as big as saucers. My partner just stared at me and rolled his eyes. My white uniform was a mess, but I was grinning from ear to ear. Best catch I ever made.

Some people liken assisting at childbirth to being a catcher more than a medical person. But knowing what signs to look for in the mom and baby, being able to recognize and reverse potentially injurious or fatal complications, turn these calls into more than a casual aside. Many moms are very prepared and experienced in childbirth, especially if it's not their first baby. One morning at the end of my shift at 7:00 a.m. when I was working as a paramedic in Santa Maria, California, the relief crew was late when a call came in. Of course, that meant that my EMT partner Steve and I would have to work overtime. But instead of the usual "woman in labor" call, the Dispatch called over the radio, "Baby being born." Now that got our juices flowing and, without even putting on my uniform shirt, (I was wearing a t-shirt that I had been sleeping in and usually wore under my uniform shirt), we rushed to the ambulance, put our seatbelts on and responded to the call.

As we pulled up to the apartment complex, a man was waving wildly at us in the middle of the street. I grabbed the jump box and ALS bag, and Steve followed with the rest of the equipment.

The fire engine, which responds to all medical calls, was a few minutes behind us. I entered the apartment complex and ran up two flights of stairs, behind the man who had waved us down. It turned out he was the dad. As I entered the bedroom, I saw a blonde woman on a bed with her legs up and apart, and trying so very hard to breathe but not to push. She looked strained. She was soaked and I thought she must have been working hard. I introduced myself as I entered the room and looked around, then between her legs. The infant's head was straining against the surrounding area called the perineum. Sometimes births could be so explosive that the perineum can tear. These are sometimes only small tears, but at other times they can rip clear through to the rectum.

When a baby drops into the lower pelvic area to be born, not only does the cervix and vagina have to widen to five or more inches, but also the tunnel that is the cervix has to flatten like a pancake. This is called effacement. Babies' heads are huge and with all the pushing, once the head is through, the rest can follow like a shot. It can cause damage to nerves and trauma to the baby and mom. So one of my jobs was to try to prevent an explosive delivery.

I knelt on the bed and placed my left hand on the crown of the baby's head, still straining hard against the perineum, which was stretched very tight. As the contraction subsided, the mom fought to catch her breath, and I slipped my fingers into the effaced area of her perineum and began to gently pull up, out and down, a maneuver that may help stretch the perineum and prevent tearing. As I did this, I began to smell cigarette smoke. I looked up to see the dad with a newly lit cigarette in his mouth.

"Hey!" I called to him. "Out with that."

As if he just realized what he was doing, he pulled it out of his mouth with a start and darted out of the room. He returned a minute later, with a camera. His wife and the mother-to-be, Barbara, glared at him and said, "You better take proper pictures!" He assured her he would. Then she pushed again. I again applied even pressure to the crown of the baby's head as it began to ease out through the vulva. First his eyes, then nose and mouth followed with the smallest of 'pops' as the head cleared the mother. Steve had the bulb syringe ready for me as I supported the head and allowed it to rotate to accommodate the following shoulder. I pushed the bulb into its mouth to suction out fluids. I followed with the nostrils, then back to the mouth. He was grayish but not blue, and his eyes were still closed. Almost without warning, the rest of the baby began to slip from the mother. The shoulders, arms, torso, buttocks and legs followed with ease. I held him and saw the glistening white and lavender umbilical cord. I held the baby low, level with the pelvis and called out, "It's a boy!"

The dad let out a whoop, mom cried and, for good measure, the baby joined in. I clamped the umbilical cord in two places, wiped the crying baby with a clean towel and handed him naked to his mom. He was gorgeous. She took him in her arms and held him tightly to her breast. She looked up to the ceiling with closed eyes and then opened them to look down to her son.

She looked at me and said, "His name is Christopher. We have been hoping for a boy after two girls."

"Hi Christopher," I said.

Steve and I took vital signs on the mom and wrapped the baby up and gave him back to her. She was very weak so we piled her onto the gurney and brought her down the stairs to the ambulance. John, the dad, kept taking pictures. The placenta hadn't delivered and Barbara hadn't resumed the contractions needed to expel it, so we headed off to the hospital at a safe pace. On the way, I asked John if he wanted to cut the umbilical cord.

His face lit up and he said, "Can I?"

"Sure," I responded. I handed him the sterile scissors and showed him where to cut. Once that was done I said, "Christopher, you're on your own."

Barbara continued to do well, but I couldn't help asking her how she, an experienced mom, had missed the signs of delivery, resulting in a home birth.

It certainly wasn't her plan, she replied. She had taken a shower and apparently her water broke during the shower. Because she was wet, she didn't notice. When she went into labor, she thought she had plenty of time, thinking the amniotic sac was still intact. It came as quite a shock when the contractions picked up and the baby started to crown. That's when they called 911. I secretly thanked my lucky stars for that shower … it gave me a chance to help with another special delivery.

One afternoon at Lodgepole, in Sequoia National Park, I received a call from Ranger Tom to respond to a cabin at Pinewood in the Giant Forest. At that time, Pinewood was employee housing for the park concessionaire. Rangers Ginny and Rita also responded. The call was for a woman in labor. At cabin 532, we pulled up and the dry dirt lifted into the air. I entered the one-room cabin which was made, in part, of old giant sequoia wood. It was a relic of the early days in Giant Forest and it looked it. The room was dominated by a double bed and there was little room to maneuver. A tall, thin man introduced me to his wife Laura who was lying on the bed, partially propped up by two pillows. She was 22 years old, had dark stringy hair and looked miserable. Her face was puffy and pale and she appeared to be grimacing as a contraction swept over her. She was in active labor.

Our team set out to stabilize and transport Laura. I spoke to her and she was not very forthcoming. I later realized she just didn't know the answers to my many questions.

"How far along are you?" I asked.

"I don't know," she replied.

"Okay, then when was your last menstrual period?" I asked.

Again, "I don't know," was her reply.

Her blood pressure was dangerously high for a pregnant woman, 150/92. Plasma volume increases by 50% during pregnancy. Along with the new blood supply to the uterus, there is a natural drop in blood pressure during pregnancy. So a systolic of 150 heralded a potentially hazardous situation. I did a head-to-toe examination and noted that, in addition to her puffy face, her legs were swollen. By pressing a finger into her lower calf, I blanched the skin and it took a long time to return to its normal position. This was pitting edema and sealed the diagnosis. Laura had pregnancy-induced hypertension (PIH) which can lead to eclampsia, a dangerous condition that causes seizures and coma in pregnant women. Electrolyte imbalances were difficult to reverse and sustained seizures, status epilepticus, could cause grave harm to the mother and, perhaps, prove fatal to an unborn baby. Flashing lights, loud noises and other stimuli can set off the seizures. In addition, time was not on my side. She needed to be in a hospital now and we were two hours from the ER in Fresno. She needed to fly.

But if we flew, could the loud noise of the motor and the

whirling pattern of the rotors stimulate her to seize? I thought she would seize one way or the other and, at least, it was a shorter trip by helicopter. I asked Tom to order one up to Red Fir, our LZ about six miles away.

During my exam, I listened for fetal heart tones and movement but heard and felt none. I examined her vulva privately and noted she was dilated just a bit with little effacement. As I talked to Laura more, she had no idea how far along she was and had had no prenatal care. I guessed her at about six to seven months. She also admitted to two other pregnancies, but both ended in abortions without complications.

By the time we were ready to move her, I had established an IV in her hand, rather than in a joint like the AC (antecubital) space in her arm, in case she had a seizure. She was on oxygen and she was sitting up at about forty-five degrees, a position known as semi-Fowlers. I placed a pillow under her right side to lift her more to the left, a position called left lateral, to keep the weight of her pregnancy off the great blood vessels that ran in front of her spine.

Her contractions were fifteen seconds long and about three minutes apart. I contacted my Base Station Physician (BSP) in the ER in Fresno and was ordered to give Laura a 400cc fluid challenge to try to slow the contractions. What a dilemma; I wanted to slow the contractions as I thought Laura would give birth to an unstable premature infant, or quite possibly a stillborn baby. It would be a rough resuscitation in the Bell Ranger helicopter because there was little room for the pilot, Laura and me. But I was also afraid that if I gave her any fluid bolus, it would add to her PIH and she would seize. I opened up the IV and began administration of the bolus.

At the helibase, they configured the waiting ship, while I did one last vaginal exam. Things had changed quickly. I could now see a crowning head, and the cervix had dilated to about seven centimeters with increased effacement. I recontacted the BSP and was ordered to wait ten minutes in case the delivery happened, but the bolus must have worked and, after ten minutes, there was no change.

We loaded Laura into the helicopter with her facing toward the rear of the ship, propped up on the long board with a seatbelt diagonally across her chest. (Most patients have their head to the rear of the ship and their feet forward.) I was in an adjacent seat facing forward, about parallel with Laura's knees. I had my emergency OB kit ready. We hung the IV bag up and secured the oxygen tank that fed Laura the oxygen through a nasal cannula at six liters per minute. I looked up at the bright blue sky and saw the rotors begin to turn. I had Valium standing by in case she seized, but magnesium sulfate would have been better. Magnesium sulfate was not a pre-hospital care medication at that time. I took Laura's hand and assured her she would be okay. She squeezed it tightly. Once we lifted off, I palpated another blood pressure. I was excited to see it was now down to 140 systolic with a pulse of 116 and respirations at 24. We took off and headed down the mountain.

As I turned my head to check on the amount of oxygen left in the cylinder, Laura reached out with her left foot and kicked me squarely in the shoulder. I quickly turned my head to the left, but any irritation I might have had evaporated as I saw her strain mightily with her knees widened and her head arched over her abdomen. This must have been a doozy of a contraction and she was pushing. I had taught her the short puff-like breaths to get her through her previous contractions to keep her from pushing, but she was beyond that. In between her legs was the crown of a very tiny head with light golden hair. I gently placed my left hand there and the head came out in one easy slip. I helped the oh-so-tiny infant rotate to accommodate the shoulders. The pushing stopped as I picked up the bulb syringe and began suctioning and resuscitation. The baby's eyes were closed and it did not stir. I slipped the syringe between her lips and pulled out a mouthful of mucous and repeated this with the nose. Strangely, I noted, the baby wasn't as blue as I had expected. I suctioned the mouth again and, as we passed over Reedley, a hearty, albeit tiny, cry came from the baby's mouth. She's alive!

I suctioned more vigorously and the baby cried louder. The pilot turned around wide-eyed and took in the scene. And what a scene it was. The rest of the baby slipped out. She was a small, small girl, barely five pounds. She appeared to have no fat on her and was a miniature baby. But, by golly, she knew how to cry. Laura smiled in relief and closed her eyes as I held her little girl, drying her and suctioning her. I figured that as long as the umbilical cord was attached and working, the baby was receiving oxygenated blood from the mother who still had the nasal cannula for oxygen. I kept the baby level with Laura's heart to prevent an unusual shift in blood from the baby to mom, or vice versa. Much to my surprise, we landed within minutes of the baby's completed entrance into the world. There was a neonatal team waiting and a doctor jumped on board. We clamped and cut the cord and the tiny baby was handed down in her ambulance sheet to the waiting incubator. Then Laura was lifted out. I accompanied her into the ER and reported the situation. I was a mess, with amniotic fluid and bloody fluids of birth on my shirt and arms. But I wasn't half as bad as the helicopter. It was a real mess. Fluids had dribbled and dripped down to the floor and cracks below the birth area.

Before we headed back to Ash Mountain to clean up the helicopter, I went in to say goodbye to Laura. The baby was already in the neonatal intensive care unit. Laura gave me a hug and said she had named her baby, Veronica Nancy. I was so proud and pleased.

When I went outside, the pilot had reconfigured the helicopter and we headed to the park for clean up. It was fun to talk about what happened, and we debated about the place of birth to put on the birth certificate. The head came out over Reedley, but the rest came out over Fresno!

Just before we landed, Dispatch radioed and said I needed to call the ER in Fresno immediately upon landing. My smile went away. My first thought was that Veronica had died. She was so tiny. I darted to the phone after landing and called the ER.

"Is everything okay?" I asked.

"The baby and mom are fine," the nurse replied. "But the mom has tested positive for Hepatitis-B and you need to come down for a blood test and a shot of gamma globulin."

I was relieved at the news that all were okay, but realized that this job was potentially dangerous in so many ways. From a helicopter flight to a microscopic virus, you never know what the next danger might be. So you were always prepared, wearing gloves and masks and all other protective equipment.

After the cleanup, I went to Visalia to the small hospital there, had my blood drawn and got a shot in my butt. I never got Hepatitis, thank goodness, but I did have a great memory of the little girl who was bound and determined to make a spectacular entrance into this world.

TATTOO

What a day. It was my third medical evacuation from the canyon and the clinic was thinking of putting me on the payroll for all the patients I was bringing to them. I was hiding in the x-ray room trying to catch up on my paperwork when Mike, the shift supervisor, stuck his head around the corner with that smile he gets on his face when he is about to add to your workload.

"Want to go to a call at Desert View to a man shot in the hand?"

"The hand," I thought. "At least it will be uncomplicated."

"Which hand?" I asked as I rose up from the desk contemplating all of the unfinished paperwork.

"Not the hand," Mike replied, "the head. He's been shot in the head."

He was so calm about it all. But the thought of the call re-energized me and I made a beeline to the clinic door and my patrol car, and headed for the helibase.

It was a short flight to Desert View, and the capable EMTs there had packaged the patient with full spinal precautions, placed him on oxygen and strapped him into the ambulance. I jumped out of the helicopter with my medical bag and jogged across the open dirt of the LZ and into the back of the ambulance. The EMTs said that three local men had been hunting on the reservation adjacent to the park. They had been drinking heavily when one man raised his rifle, pointed it at the patient and pulled the trigger. With a "BOOM," the projectile tore into the man's skull and down he went. His friends threw him into the back of a pickup truck and drove him to the Desert View entrance station and asked for help. The man who shot him said it had been an accident and that the patient had stepped into his line of fire as he was pulling the trigger. This would all get sorted out later. For now, there was a man with a severe head injury.

A large male was lying on the backboard with a bandage on this head and a non-rebreather oxygen mask over his face. His eyes were closed as I began to set up an IV. I put my medical gloves on and carefully lifted the bandage off of his head. Underneath there was no scalp, no skin and no skull. Like hitting a coconut just right, a piece of his skull about three inches long by two inches high had been scooped from his head. Underneath was an anatomy lesson. The ivory white lobes and convolutions of the brain could be seen in this window with the blood vessels pulsating on the surface.

I wanted to know if I had to place an advanced airway into the patient before we took off so I tried to wake him up. He did not answer when I called out his name. As I leaned over to rub my knuckles on his sternum, I could smell the odor of alcohol on his breath through the oxygen mask. As soon as I rubbed on his sternum, his eyes popped open.

I said, "Hi."

He said, "Hi."

I told him that I was a paramedic and that I was there to help him. I told him that he had been injured and I was taking him to the hospital at Flagstaff Medical Center. I told him I needed him to answer some quick questions for me and he said, "Okay."

"What is your full name?" I asked. He told me.

"Can you tell me what month this is?" He told me.

"Can you tell me where you are?" He wasn't sure.

"How about what happened to you?' I asked. He said he wasn't sure, but he did have a headache.

I wasn't sure how much of his hampered mental ability was injury or alcohol or both, so I asked one more question. One that would make him search his brain for an answer.

"What is your social security number?" I asked.

Without hesitation, he raised his right forearm to his eyes and correctly recited his social security number. I was astonished, until I realized he had his social security number tattooed onto his forearm! That was a new one for me.

I quickly finished the IV, and we flew him to the emergency room without incident. I later learned he recovered fully and that he had a plate in place of the missing bone in his head. ❏

Pima Point

We were on the long final approach to the LZ at Pima Point when something hit the helicopter ... and hit it hard. The pilot Jerry later said it was wind shear. Whatever it was, it shoved the helicopter as if it had been hit by a giant hand and drove it toward the ground. As it began to hurtle toward the earth, the occupants of the aircraft felt their stomachs go into their mouth as if they were in a runaway elevator. Jim and I didn't have that luxury. We were outside of the helicopter, hanging beneath it on the shorthaul rope. As the helicopter fell downward, I looked up to see the underbelly of the Bell Long Ranger career toward us as our rope became slack by the uneven fall of the chopper and the puny humans below it. It truly happened so suddenly that I didn't have time to react, at first.

As we plummeted to the ground I reached up and grabbed the rope with both hands and then looked down. Just then, the rope became taut, and we were jerked up and thrown around like someone on a bungee cord. We settled under the rope, slowly rocking under the helicopter that had stopped its fall with Jerry's great reactions to the unplanned near-disaster. I looked over at Jim who stared back at me with open mouth and wide eyes. I actually heard the expletive that came from his lips over the wind and roar of the helicopter engine. I laughed in relief, and blurted out, "Oh boy!"

Within a few minutes we were slowly lowered to the pavement at the Pima Point overlook and, with shaky legs, unclipped and walked away from the helicopter. Several people came up to us. One gave me a hug and said, "Are you all right?"

"I think so," I smiled in reply.

"Wow!" someone else said. "You fell close to sixty feet. It's a good thing you weren't over pavement or you'd have been splattered!"

Now that was a mental picture I hadn't contemplated. I had about five thousand feet of canyon between the ground and me. But I admitted we had been lucky. I'd been lucky since the beginning of this mission. It started the day before for us, but actually, it began several months before for others.

Pima Point is on West Rim Drive. It's a delightful eight-mile one-way road to Hermit's Rest and the beginning of the Hermit Trail into the canyon. The Hermit's Rest area was designed by Fred Harvey Company architect Mary Elizabeth Jane Coulter, and has a huge fireplace and a feeling of antiquity about it. The road is closed to private cars in the summer months due to the lack of parking spaces. A free shuttle bus takes folks to the various stops along the way. In the winter, the road is open to private cars due to the decrease in the number of tourists. We patrolled it as often as we could. Many nights in the winter, our shift only had enough time to patrol to Maricopa or Hopi Points, the most visited overlooks. Getting as far as the Abyss, Pima Point or Hermit's Rest was an exception, not the rule. The Abyss is an intimidating overlook. It is truly straight down for thousands of feet to the first stop at the bottom of huge cliffs. Pima Point farther to the west is more isolated. It is reached by a short loop road and is so close to Hermit's Rest that it is often bypassed. The cliffs are also very intimidating at Pima Point, but they slope out more. You can hit ground at six hundred feet, go down a slant, go three hundred more, and then another several hundred. It is more of a stair step than a sheer face.

* * * *

Before this particular mission, Pima Point had been the scene of another serious call. It was winter and so cars were allowed to drive out and park. I worked the night shift in winter. Often the roads were icy or the call volume so high in the Village at Grand Canyon that we never had an opportunity to make it all the way to Hermit's Rest. The night before this at 10:00 p.m., Ranger Kim had gone as far as Hopi Point and back. The next day she would chide herself for not driving farther. A folding stool, an empty bottle of vodka and a flashlight were all at Pima Point. There was a rope tied to the railing and a business card with a note belonging to a 33-year-old male named Mark.

The note stated: "I'm dead, call the Rangers."

The Rangers were called.

Attached to the rope at the railing was a HK .308 assault rifle. Tangled in the rope and hanging over the cliff at Pima Point was Mark. He had apparently shot himself with the rifle and, in his fall, became entangled in the rope. It was a mystery why the rifle was tied to the railing and not the deceased, until we found the six-page suicide note. The deceased was addicted to heroin and other drugs. He just couldn't face life anymore and intended to kill himself. He said he wanted his best friend to have his rifle after he was gone. This explained why it was tied to the railing. (I don't know about you, but I would not want a gift of the rifle that my best friend used to kill himself. Sigh.)

* * * *

On May 8th at 3:49 p.m., the day before we fell 60 feet attached to the bottom of the helicopter, a citizen reported a vehicle over the edge just east of Pima Point. Ranger Keith and others responded, and Keith quickly set up to rappel to the car, because it was too windy to fly the helicopter. The 1993 maroon Nissan rental was located 600 feet below the rim. Keith rappelled down 450 feet and hiked another 150 feet to the car's location. He noted it was very smashed and on its roof. The slope was a steep angle here, and the car hadn't continued any farther into the canyon because a sturdy pinyon pine had blocked it on the slope. Keith confirmed there was a "901" present. ("901" is radio code for a dead body.) He also confirmed the body had been there quite some time, perhaps weeks, by the presence of insects and the odor of decay. Keith ascended the cliff and plans were made for a technical Search and Rescue (SAR) for the next day that would involve the helicopter if the wind and other factors were within flight parameters.

Many people believe the movie "Thelma and Louise" was filmed at the Grand Canyon. It wasn't, but within a short time of its debut we had a few drive-off suicides in the park. One young man went to the South Kaibab Trailhead parking lot and attempted to drive off the 400-foot cliff. He hit a rock, backed up, hit another rock, backed up and then finally succeeded in driving off the cliff to his death. I know people who do these things are despondent, but someone has to go in for the remains. It's what we do in our culture. But in the past, they were not always successful in getting the cars out.

People have been driving off of the canyon for decades. I don't know of any that were accidental. One Ranger who worked here before I did told me that on several occasions, when cars drove off and folks died, they went down and collected the remains. But there were no helicopters strong enough and affordable enough to haul the cars out. He told me Rangers went down later and sprayed the cars with paint to help them blend in with the rocks. I wonder.

But in my time, heavy-lift helicopters did have the capability to raise cars out of the canyon to the 7,000-foot elevation. Usually the rental company or vehicle insurance carrier picked up the bill. That was the plan with this Pima Point vehicle.

The next morning just after 7:00 a.m., we began the SAR. We not only needed technical rescue and shorthaul specialists, but also fire brigade members. Once we got to the vehicle, we would have to use the Hurst Tool (or "Jaws of Life") to open the car to remove the remains. As a result, folks who had never shorthauled before were given a quick in-service and allowed to fly, as long as they were with a certified technical shorthaul specialist. I was one of those specialists and Ranger Jim would join me for his first flight.

Chuck and Dave flew before Jim and me. We were prepared to spend the day, doing a very dirty job. In addition to water, food and survival gear, we had coveralls and masks we would wear. To dull the smell of decay, I put Vicks Vapo-Rub in my mask. It helped a little. We also had our structural firefighting helmets, gloves and goggles. Later, extrication tools would be sent to us in a cargo net under the helicopter. Jim and I waited off to the side for our shorthaul. We checked all of our equipment. We double-checked our seat and shoulder harnesses and the two lines that we would clip into the ring on the rope below the helicopter. We checked that our flight suit leg and arm zippers and Velcro were closed, collars were up, eye-protection in place, and helmets secured. I had a backpack of gear and equipment, and reviewed signals with Jim. I would do the marshalling and signaling, and he would fly along. We waited for Doug to call the Bell Long Ranger over to the closed Pima Point parking lot. It did a hover check, with the spotter in the back seat of the helicopter leaning out to look at the ground, while the pilot Jerry held hover. Doug gave us the okay to approach and the three of us walked to the rope. A few feet of the rope lay on the ground along with the attached ten-pound weight. I constantly looked up to the under-belly of the aircraft as I walked below. Should it have a rotor or compressor failure, it could fall out of the sky like a grand piano. By keeping an eye on the underbelly, I might have a split second to react if it fell and we'd be able to jump to one side or another.

I picked up the end of the rope and quickly clipped my two harness carabiners into the ring. Jim quickly followed, and Doug stepped out of the way as I tapped the top of my helmet to signal okay, then made a lifting motion with my left arm to communicate we were ready to lift off. Within seconds we were airborne and, in no time, went from thirty feet off the ground to thousands of feet as we flew off of Pima Point and over the Grand Canyon. It was a quick flight, just a few minutes. We were set down on a small flat area adjacent and upslope of the car. We quickly unclipped and, after exchanging signals, Jerry flew off for more fuel and supplies.

The car was sideways against a tree on a thirty-degree slope. It was on its roof, wheels up, and the roof was smashed down to the seat tops. The driver's side was upslope, but I learned upon a quick inspection that the driver had not worn his seatbelt and was now in the passenger's side on the downslope side of the car. I also noted, as an afterthought, that the airbags had deployed. While on the downslope side of the car, I was able to get a glimpse of the remains. There was mold on his denim pants and his extremities were dried and leathery with obvious decomposition. Unfortunately, he hadn't been totally mummified. His body fluids had created a breeding ground. The odor of decay was overwhelming and there were maggots (fly larvae) all over the deceased's torso and head.

I worked my way back up to our little LZ and we confirmed our action plan. We would work solely to get the body out, put it in a body bag, and then airlift it to the South Rim Helibase where it would be turned over to the Coconino County Coroner. It was getting warm, but with car oil, fuel and body fluids running loose, we still put on our coveralls. Our radio contact was Kent (married to the other female paramedic), who was tied into a safety line so that he could lean over and see us with binoculars to radio relay for us. I don't recall when he told us, but we learned fairly early on that the deceased, prior to his death, had been despondent ever since his diagnosis as HIV positive, and suffered with AIDS. There had been no suicide notes found in the early investigation, but we realized we needed to be cautious around the corpse.

Chuck and Jim began cutting into the car after we took the

time to anchor it to the canyon and the tree. It was just after noon when we took a quick break. We wanted to finish, but we needed to get away from the fluids, maggots, stink and heat for a while, too. Dave was charting the fall line and completing the on-scene investigation with my assistance. Apparently, the car was driven off the cliff so that it hit sixteen feet out, away from the cliff face after first hitting about 240 feet down. It was on a roll, literally, until it hit that little tree 600 feet down and finally came to a stop. Otherwise, it would have gone hundreds, even a thousand feet more, perhaps never to be discovered.

By 1400 hours, we were close to collecting the body. The car had been cut so that a release of the door would allow us to open it and roll the body gently downhill into the body bag. With my mask, helmet, eye protection and coveralls on, I worked my way about ten feet below the door and spread the body bag out. I unzipped it and spread it open, ready to pick it up and carry it to the car once the door was open. The guys on the car were getting ready to open the door when a loud metallic "snap" and "crunch" sound pealed from the car. The door sprung open and the body burst out of the car, rolling downhill and right at me. I held the body bag as high upslope as I could above me and emitted an involuntary yell as body, fluids and maggots all flew toward me. The deceased landed against the bag and knocked my legs out from under me as I rolled over the top of the bag and the body. I dug my toes in, determined not only to keep the body from rolling any further, but to keep me there, too! We stopped after a two-foot slide and I knelt back on my knees and looked up at the car. The guys were aghast. No one expected the body to spring from the car like something out of a horror movie. Within seconds of realizing everyone was okay, we all burst out in nervous laughter. Then the radio crackled. It was radio-relay Kent.

"Umm, Nancy?" he asked. "Is everything okay down there? We all just heard a very loud yell from your work area," he called.

Since I was the only gal, he knew a woman's yell when he heard it. I clicked on my radio in my chest harness and answered him, with one hand still holding the body bag over the deceased, and me on my knees dug in to hold us in place.

"10-4, we are all okay," I replied. 'We just had a sudden encounter we weren't expecting. I'll fill you in later."

By this time the guys were all around the deceased and me. We used our gloved hands to gently put the rest of the remains in the bag, and zipped it up with our rubber gloves inside. We then carried it up the slope to the LZ and placed it in the cargo net for extrication to the coroner. At 2:47 p.m., the 901 was airlifted out of the canyon. We then began our scene clean up and prepared equipment in cargo nets that would precede us. It was on this flight out that Jerry was hit by a downdraft and Jim and I had our freefall from hell. What a day.

Later in July, a salvage helicopter, a Sikorsky S-58T Heavy Lift, arrived to remove the car. Rangers again shorthauled down to the vehicle and secured lift lines to the vehicle. It was carried out gently, in contrast to its violent fall of many months before. It was taken to the storage area and later removed by trailer from the park.

RON

Larry's paramedic partner, Ron, was a smart paramedic. But he could also be a pain. His humor was off the wall. Once he bought some gummy bears and showed me a blue one and bit it in half.

"Look, I'm biting the heads off of blue babies," he laughed.

"Ron, you are a sick man," I responded and walk away, sighing.

But he loved his two Golden Retrievers and he was a patient partner to Larry and he helped me learn a lot.

After I graduated from paramedic school, I worked seasonally for a private ambulance company in the San Francisco Bay Area, and later in Stanislaus and Santa Barbara Counties in California. Ron was often my partner, and we had a ton of calls on the 101 Freeway that ran south of the city. One afternoon on my day off, I received a call. I sat down as I listened.

Ron and Dave were working the 101 Freeway ambulance and received a call to respond to a collision on the four-lane, south-bound 101. They positioned the ambulance behind the flare pattern that had been set up by the CHP (California Highway Patrol). Two cars had sideswiped each other. One was against the railing at the median, the other in front of the CHP vehicle ahead of the flare pattern. It was just after noon, and the CHP had slowed traffic so that it was flowing slowly through the collision scene. Dave went to the car on the right and Ron to the one on the left at the median. Dave called over that his patient seemed okay. Because the driver's door of the other car was against the median, Ron stuck his head into the passenger window of the sedan. The female patient was alert and oriented and a bit shaken up. Ron called over to Dave that he thought his patient was okay, too. Ron stuck his head back into the passenger window to continue to assess the patient.

A whirring sound coupled with a loud thumping began to get louder as it approached from the north. The CHP officer and Dave looked up just in time to see a sedan, traveling at a very high rate of speed, careen through the accident scene, creating that weird sound as it drove through the flare pattern, spinning flares off in all directions. They watched in horror as the speeding sedan hit Ron full on as he stood looking into the passenger window of the accident car on the median. The woman driver of the accident car screamed as Ron's head hit the edge of the open window frame and his face and part of his head were sheared off onto her lap. The officer and Dave raced over to Ron's body; blood gushing from his partially severed head. Dave ran back and grabbed the gurney from the ambulance. They threw Ron's body on it, sped it back, and put it in the back of the ambulance. Without any attendant, Dave sped off of the freeway to the nearest ER. He pulled in shouting and yelling. Nurses and attendants poured out of the ER to the ambulance bay and they brought the lifeless body into the trauma room. No one recognized Ron. The doctor walked in, took one look and pronounced the body dead. Dave screamed that it was Ron. The trauma team looked closer. Through the blood they saw a hint of what was left of Ron's paramedic uniform. They all had known him. They covered him up and led Dave out of the room.

Did I forget to mention that the car that hit and killed Paramedic Ron was operated by a drunk driver? ❏

JAIL BAIT

I started my shift early on the South Rim at 6:00 a.m. It was a gorgeous warm morning. By 7:15 a.m. I had fed the horses, driven to the usual illegal camp spots and looked at the beauty of the Grand Canyon, with the long morning shadows the buttes threw on the far walls with the rising sun. Dispatch called and stated the dining room manager at the Maswik Cafeteria wanted to report a suspicious person: a possible escaped convict! That is definitely not an ordinary call. I was only minutes away. I parked out front and walked in past the tourists through the automatic door and into the lobby. The registration desk was to my left and the gift store to my right. The dining room was straight ahead with an east and west section split by the cafeteria serving area in the middle. As I neared the tray and silverware area, John, the morning manager, approached.

"I think there is an escaped con in the dining room," he said.

I was a bit skeptical and asked him what made him think so.

"He's dressed in jail coveralls and eating like a horse!" he replied.

I walked to the wall that allowed me a peek into the east dining room. There, sitting at a table by himself, was a man with brown hair who looked to be in his early twenties. He was bent over a tray of food and eating ravenously. He was in a full body coverall that was a bright orange. Across the back, written in black, were four capital letters representing a jail facility in an adjoining state to Arizona. Down each of his pant legs in bold black capital letters was the word, JAIL. I hadn't expected the call to be real and I didn't expect the clues to be so obvious.

I asked John to keep a discreet eye on the suspect as I stepped back a few feet and called in to Dispatch and asked for backup. I asked another Ranger to wait outside the east dining room door and one to meet me in the lobby. When all were in place, we would take the suspect quietly outside (we hoped) and go from there. I didn't want a scene in the dining room and I didn't know how desperate an escaped convict might be, especially with lots of potential hostages and knives and forks all around.

When Ranger Marty radioed he was in place, Ranger Mike and I walked into the dining room to proceed with the plan we had discussed in the lobby. I approached the suspect on the right and Mike came up on his left.

I leaned over slightly and said quietly, "Police officers; don't move and please keep your hands where we can see them."

The suspect froze. I instructed him to put down his knife and fork slowly and then to slowly stand up to walk outside. He complied as we seamlessly escorted him out the northeast glass door. There, Mike quickly searched him while Marty provided cover. He had no pockets, no identification and no weapons. I had him sit on the ground with his back against the wall. I asked him to identify himself and he gave me his name and date of birth. I called it in to Dispatch to check for wants and warrants. Then I asked him what he was doing here in the Grand Canyon with jail fatigues on. He seemed nervous but gave a hint of a smile.

"I just got hired as a GRA (Guest Room Attendant) and I work later today. I came over to have breakfast."

"What is with the jail clothes?" I said.

He said he bought them at a swap meet and used them as pajamas and lounging clothes. He just woke up and walked over to have breakfast in them.

When Dispatch radioed that the suspect was clear of wants or warrants, I asked her to call the facility on the jail coveralls and ask if anyone was missing and if they could account for any missing jail outfits. In the meantime, the Fire and Safety Officer, who was the security for the concessionaire and part of the park's emergency response team, confirmed that the suspect was indeed a new hire and lived in one of the motor lodge cabins. Dispatch then called and asked if I could get to a phone. I left the suspect with Mike and Marty and went into the manager's office. Dispatch called and said they had a corrections officer (CO) from the jail on the line. The CO said they had all their prisoners accounted for. I asked if he could explain their jail's coveralls on this person. He sheepishly said that they often dispose of old coveralls by giving them to charitable groups, and some do end up at swap meets.

"Don't you see a problem with this?" I asked him. "Isn't the whole point of being bright orange with JAIL written all the over the outfit to help officers and others identify them as convicts? If they became casual wear, how would we identify the good guys from the escaped bad guys?"

"I do now," he replied. "This has never come up before, and we will get right on this to keep it from happening again." The CO thanked me and hung up.

I went back to the suspect and told him his story matched. We walked him back to his room to check his identification. I strongly suggested to him that, while he could wear the coveralls, he should not leave his room with them on or he might again be mistaken for an escaped convict. He agreed to keep them as inside clothes in the future. ❑

Danny Ray

One of the many nice things about living in the West is the culture. I have always been an outdoors gal and love the western lifestyle. When we moved to Grand Canyon, we discovered a community about three hours away that held a rodeo each year. The town was Prescott, Arizona, and they boasted that they had the oldest rodeo in the west. Unfortunately for my husband Kent and me, the rodeo was held on the 4th of July. We always worked the 4th unless it fell on our days off. We really liked the Prescott area; its old-town ambience with craft fairs, parades and cowboy poetry competitions. We often met our friends, Joe and Rose, and went through the antique stores. In 1992, Kent and I were excited to discover that this year our lieu days included the 4th of July. Not only did I get tickets for the rodeo, but I also secured a hotel room for us, an almost impossible feat.

On May 12th of that same year, a convict, Danny Ray, was serving four consecutive life sentences for a 1991 bank robbery in Winslow, Arizona. He was to be extradited to California to be tried for the 1990 murder and dismemberment of a man there. On this day, wearing a lab coat, he walked out of the prison. Dog teams and helicopters searched for him but did not locate him. On June 3rd he was spotted in a campground in northeast Arizona but he eluded authorities again. They did not pick up his trail again until June 11th, when they found a cabin Danny Ray had burglarized, and they learned the description of a truck he had stolen. He abandoned the truck on June 21st in the Coconino National Forest. All this was news to us, but on June 25th, it became a reality.

Danny Ray kidnapped a couple in Flagstaff, Arizona, and forced them to drive to the Grand Canyon. After spending the night in a hotel, Danny Ray kept them with him in their vehicle the rest of the day. At 9:15 p.m., in the twilight of the 26th, Ranger Donnie was in the General Store parking lot when a young boy ran up to him.

"You've got to stop him. He's taking my dad. He's kidnapping my family!" the youngster cried.

Donnie looked to the east side of the parking lot where there was a small group of people talking outside of a recreational vehicle (RV). Donnie got into his patrol car and called for back-up. As he drove toward the group, the boy called out, "He's got a gun."

Donnie pulled up behind a car that the suspect, later identified as Danny Ray, was standing adjacent to. Donnie stepped out of his vehicle and ordered Danny Ray to step toward him. Danny Ray turned toward Donnie and pointed a revolver at him. Donnie took cover in his vehicle and pulled his pistol. Aware of all of the bystanders in the area, Donnie was cautious with his weapon. Danny Ray got into his hijacked car with the kidnapped couple and drove at a high rate of speed toward the Yavapai Lodge. As Danny Ray pulled onto South Entrance Road, Rangers John and Chris were together in a patrol car just pulling in. Danny Ray shot at them as Donnie pulled up behind the suspect vehicle. Ranger Keith arrived and tried to force Danny Ray's vehicle into a ditch, but he was able to get around the Ranger's cruiser and head toward the West Rim. Donnie continued to follow the suspect as the other two patrol cars turned around to follow. Dispatch sounded a General Alarm for all law enforcement officers. We all began to respond.

At the West Rim interchange, Danny Ray rammed the railroad gate and broke the post. As Donnie followed, Danny Ray brandished his revolver out his window. It was almost dark as the patrol cars followed the suspect vehicle past Hopi Point. Just around a corner, Danny Ray braked, jumped out of the car and bolted to the south side of the road into the forest. The Rangers took defensive cover as they parked their vehicles behind the suspect car. They didn't know if the two persons remaining in the car were victims or suspects. Coconino County Sheriff Deputies Jim and Brett joined the Rangers on the scene at West Rim. They identified the suspect car occupants as kidnap victims and thus began the manhunt for Danny Ray.

Officers from a multitude of agencies poured into the Grand Canyon. They included the Coconino County Sheriff's Department, Federal Bureau of Investigation (FBI), U.S. Park Police, Flagstaff Police Department, Arizona Department of Public Safety (DPS), United States Forest Service and more. Over 300 officers eventually descended on the Grand Canyon for this manhunt. That night, officers attempted to contain Danny Ray to the south-side forest. What was not known at the time was that he had taken his boots and socks off, put his boots back on and then his socks over his boots. This minimized the tracks he made. In the dark, he crossed over to the north side of the road and made his way back east toward the village area. He had left an audiotape behind in the hijacked car. With his plan to kidnap the family of six in the market parking lot, he was prepared to demand one million dollars and the release of his brother who was incarcerated in Florence Prison.

A decision was made by administrators not to close the park to tourists. All Ranger leaves were cancelled. All days off were erased. All Rangers reported for duty to be assigned roles in the manhunt. I had a dual role. There were still local calls and medical responses for Grand Canyon. I worked with several imported paramedics from Phoenix to cover the medical response. I was also a liaison for the FBI Hostage Rescue Team (HRT) on site. We met in the local high school auditorium where the incident command had established the commissary area. NPS employees Jerry and Karyn were there. They worked at the helibase and we were arranging helicopter orientation flights of both the village and the immediate canyon area for the HRT members.

The next day, Pilot Jerry and I took HRT members, a few at a time, on these orientation flights. I was the running commentary. I pointed out the buildings, roads, trails and more. When it came to dropping into the canyon from the Abyss, I sensed Jerry looking at me. He smiled and I smiled. As he went over the rim, he dove steeply into the canyon with a stomach-in-your-mouth effect, announcing over the intraship communications: "Welcome to the Grand Canyon." Every single one of those HRT guys yelled like they were on a roller coaster and thought it was the best part of the whole assignment. Jerry was a quiet guy, but he had a devil-side to him at times.

* * * *

I worked with the paramedics from Phoenix on a variety of calls. They were professional and competent. It was a definite change of pace for them from city calls, and they told me they liked being more on their own, with their improvisational skills being challenged. The next morning at 10:00 a.m., Dispatch reported a man with chest pain about a mile below the rim on the Bright Angel Trail. The Phoenix medics were on another call, so I threw my paramedic bag on my back, grabbed a cylinder of oxygen and began to run down the trail. With my body armor, flight suit and defensive equipment on, I got pretty hot. I arrived on scene to find a 63-year-old male named Bob with shortness of breath and clutching his chest. I immediately called for more resources, in between catching my breath and stripping my flight suit to my waist and removing my body armor. It was over 100 degrees Fahrenheit already! I spoke to Bob, reassured him, placed him on oxygen and started an IV. Others arrived with the heart monitor and I confirmed the EKG changes that indicated a possible heart attack. He received aspirin, nitroglycerin and morphine as we waited for the wheeled litter and carry teams to reach us. His chest pain was mostly relieved with the treatment. When I heard the boot poundings of the arriving backup, I couldn't help but smile at the DPS Officer among them. He was in the village on an "as needed" basis. His long-sleeved uniform was crisp and clean and his flat hat with the braids was perfect. The only thing that gave him away was the sweat pouring from his temples and brows. We carried Bob to the rim in the litter. It was balanced on a single wheel. At the top he was placed in the ambulance and taken to a waiting medical helicopter at the helibase to fly him to Flagstaff Medical Center.

* * * *

Day after 12-hour day we looked for Danny Ray. At one point I told my Kent, "I'm so mad at losing the only chance we had to go to the Prescott Rodeo that I don't know if I could control myself if he came out of the woods with his hands up!" I was kidding of course . . . mostly.

On June 29th, Danny Ray stole a station wagon at gunpoint, and tried to take more hostages, but the occupants escaped. We had officers at every exit of the park, searching each vehicle. He apparently spent some time in the Search and Rescue cache, eating the Meals Ready to Eat (MRE's) and waiting for his next opportunity. I spent time at various checkpoints. I looked in trunks with my shotgun at the ready, held mirrors under RVs to check for undercarriage hiding spots, and crawled on top of tall trucks and RVs looking for the elusive Danny Ray. One day on the Desert Rim road checkpoint it was pretty hot and we were running out of water. DPS Officer Gary brought us ice water and was my hero from that day on.

On the 4th of July, Danny Ray struck again. He took two women hostage at Desert View and sat in the back seat of their sedan. He had dyed his hair and shaved somehow. The ladies didn't give him up as they went through the roadblocks. He had his gun pointed at them but hidden, and politely answered the officers' questions. He left the park south toward Williams, Arizona. He took the ladies into the woods near Williams and tied them to a tree. He then headed east on Interstate 40 toward

Flagstaff. The women managed to release themselves and report their kidnapping to authorities. On Interstate 17 south of Flagstaff, a DPS Officer spotted the stolen car and gave chase southbound. Danny Ray abandoned the car near Stoneman Lake and headed out on foot. It was dark when the dog teams began to track him into a residential area. On July 5th, Danny Ray was peacefully taken into custody. With a bloodhound barking in his face and an armed officer pointing a gun at him, he had little choice.

BUBBLES

For half of the year at Grand Canyon I worked the day shift, 8:00 a.m. to 5:00 p.m. The other half of the year I worked 5:00 p.m. to 2:00 a.m. The night shift for me started in the fall and went through the winter. The nights were dark and cold, and I was lucky when I was able to get off on time. My husband Kent was a day shift person all year round, so we left notes and took turns taking care of our Golden Retriever, Shannon. Shannon was a joy, but so very friendly, we knew she was a lousy watchdog. She'd carry the flashlight for the burglar. Nothing fazed her sunny outlook on life; she defined "joy."

One morning, I got off work at 2:30 a.m. and it was bitterly cold outside. The thermometer showed single digits (9 degrees Fahrenheit) when I got home. Despite my long johns under my uniform, I was cold. Luckily, I had an organic heater waiting for me. I came home, undressed and slipped under the warm covers, only to have Kent yelp in dismay as he felt my cold body sap his warmth. I felt bad for only a short time; I was so very cold.

The next night I was determined not to subject Kent to the shock of my cold body. I actually got off on time and quietly entered the house. I closed the bedroom door so I wouldn't wake Kent up, and then went into the bathroom and turned on the bathwater. I'd have a nice warm soak before going to bed and we would both be warm and happy. I added bubble bath and, as the water ran, went into the spare room where I changed my uniform out for my bathrobe. As I turned the corner to enter the bathroom, a wall of flying bubbles confronted me. It reminded me of an old "I Love Lucy" sitcom. Had I put too much bubblebath in the tub? As I took another step in toward the tub, I saw the cause. There, in the tub, soaked from head to tail in water and bubbles was my water dog, Shannon. She had a broad smile on her face and her tail was wagging so furiously at the thought of a bath and a swim that she frothed the bubblebath into a frenzy.

At first I was aghast. "Hey, you're in my bath. Get out right now!" I whispered in hard determination. Shannon responded by running in three tight circles of delight in the tub, splashing water and bubbles everywhere. She was beside herself with joy. Her antics softened me up as I reached over to turn off the water faucet and drain the tub. I spent the next hour drying Shannon off with towels and a hair dryer. She was so happy with all of the unexpected attention that I was warm in body and heart when I finally crawled into bed. ❏

Plains

"How do you get to be a Ranger?"

I have been asked that many times. I usually start by saying there are several types of Rangers. There are naturalists who give walks, talks, evening programs and answer questions at the desk. They are now called Interpreters to signify their role in explaining or interpreting the resource to the visitor. I never did like that term, and always referred to myself as a Ranger Naturalist when in that capacity. It reflected my knowledge, experience and education in the outdoors, and I was proud to be an observational biologist. A degree in the natural sciences is a usual requirement, being a "people person" and being someone who can speak publicly are all "musts." That doesn't mean it's easy. I once knew a very capable naturalist who got physically sick before every evening program. Once she got on stage, she was fine.

I personally have a bit of "ham" in me and like sharing things with folks. Perhaps it's the blarney in my Irish heritage. But it was also preparation. I learned much more than I needed to know for each program and reviewed and researched. That way I spoke with confidence on my subject. I also learned to say, "I don't know, but I'll try to find out."

There was training available for all interpreters, especially for new seasonals. After the initial introduction to the resource, they usually observe returning interpreters, and then put their programs together. There is a tremendous amount of time invested behind the scenes. It involves tons of reading, walking the trails, researching programs and submitting outlines. There should be goals, themes and objectives to each activity, not just a random nature hike, as fun as that is sometimes.

Interpreters often get to assist the Protection Rangers. Protection Rangers are often shorthanded, so naturalists who are available on their day off may walk trails looking for lost hikers or use first responder or EMT skills. That is how I became involved in the protection division. As a naturalist in Death Valley in the early 1980s, my EMT skills were used a lot. Many of the visitors were elderly and arrived with their pre-existing medical problems. It was frustrating to do CPR for hours on the way to the hospital in Las Vegas and not be able to do more. So I finally put myself through the accelerated six-month paramedic program at Stanford University Hospital and worked many winter seasons as a city paramedic. The call volume helped my skills immensely. I would get as many calls in a week in the city as I would in one summer season. Every summer I returned as a seasonal Ranger Naturalist in Sequoia National Park and doubled as a paramedic.

After a winter season in Hawaii at the Arizona Memorial at Pearl Harbor, I went to the Seasonal Law Enforcement Academy in Santa Rosa, California. It is no longer held there, but what an experience it was then. We lived in the country at an old juvenile detention center. Our rooms were cells with steel toilets, beds that hung from the walls on chains, and thick doors that closed with a resounding thud. We learned constitutional law, self-defense, search and seizure, evidence collecting and the proper handling of a firearm. On the weekends, we could participate in special training sessions. I went to an introductory structural firefighter course one weekend and an introductory high angle technical rescue course on another. We swam rapids and crossed Tyrolean traverses we built over the Russian River. We even went to the Bob Bondurant Driving Course for high-speed vehicle operations. I got an award for driving my car faster backward than I did forward through the obstacle course! (It's all done with mirrors). It was an incredible six weeks. I made lifelong friends, ran in the country every day and participated in some awesome ping-pong tournaments. I left realizing that I liked the variety and challenge of protection and began my transition from Ranger Naturalist to Protection Ranger.

There is a bit of a "catch-22" when it comes to working as a career permanent Ranger for the National Park Service (NPS). To apply for most permanent positions, you have to have status. To have status, you have to work in a permanent position for the U.S. Government. Today there are other ways to get status. Completing a tour with the Peace Corps is one, being a student intern is another way. But many get their status by working outside the NPS by taking a government position that is open to all candidates but confers status on the fortunate applicant who gets the job. In my case, I worked as a civilian paramedic for the Department of the Army. Once I completed that position, I had the coveted status and could apply for any career job for which I was qualified and met time-in-grade requirements. I could also work all year round as a seasonal. Seasonals are normally limited by the number of hours they can work for a park in a year. But a seasonal with status does not have a limit. It is not often that a seasonal is hired for the whole year. The seasonal time limitations are to keep the park from filling their ranks with inexpensive seasonals instead of hiring permanents who are more costly because of the benefits they receive.

I had been working year round as a seasonal at the Grand Canyon because of my status. My husband Kent had a permanent position as the Structural Fire Chief, but there was not a permanent position for me when we first moved there. So I worked six months as a seasonal Ranger Naturalist at the Yavapai Museum in the winter, and six months as a Protection Ranger on the South Rim in the summer. Openings were few and far between. Someone had to move to another park or "die" in order for a position to become open. It's a domino effect and at any one time a park can be missing 10% of their personnel in all divisions due to people moving on and then waiting for that position to be filled, which usually takes months.

Once a position is vacated, Human Resources puts out a position vacancy announcement, which is open for three to six weeks or more. They receive the applications which are often reviewed by a panel for qualified applicants. This last list is the certification list (the Cert), which has an expiration date. The list goes to the selecting official who calls peers, bosses and references. Then they talk to the applicant. Then the park has to decide if it has the money to pay for the move of the new employee. Sometimes they have to lapse a position for weeks or months to get that money together. By that time, the Cert may have expired and the entire process may have to be repeated.

When permanent positions at the Grand Canyon opened simultaneously in interpretation and in protection, I applied for both and became a career permanent employee in the protection division when they offered me a job. I have often wondered the path my career and life would have taken had I become a permanent employee in interpretation.

Protection Rangers are fairly new to the NPS. There have been gun-toting Rangers for decades, but the realization that trained officers were needed followed riots in Yosemite Valley's Stoneman Meadows on the 4th of July in 1970. By 1971, field Rangers were no longer just being issued a gun and a badge; they were going through actual training. By the time I went to permanent officer training, a Federal Law Enforcement Training Center (FLETC, pronounced "flet-see") had been established in Georgia. While my training then was eleven weeks long, current participants go for 87 training days – about five months – and have many additional months of Field Training with a Field Training Officer away from their home park.

Federal NPS personnel standards differ from individual state standards. For instance, the NPS has medical standards, not fitness standards. With most states, if you can do the job and pass the physical fitness requirements, you can stay. In the NPS, if you have a medical condition, unrelated to your ability to do the job, you're out. You must participate in the run, weight lifting, obstacle run, etc., but you don't have to pass. That, too, is changing. By and large, most Rangers stay in excellent shape because they must in order to perform their job. Running down trails, lifting gurneys and grappling with a bad guy all are taxing, so most of us take the Physical Efficiency Battery (PEB) seriously. Me especially so, because when I went to FLETC, the rule was that while field Rangers did not have to pass the PEB, the Rangers-in-training at FLETC must in order to participate in the program. There were nightmare stories of Rangers going all the way to Georgia and on their first day, thrown into the PEB. Those who did not pass were immediately sent home. That is expensive to a park and potentially career-ending to a Ranger, as you must have that training to keep your job.

So when I found out I was going to FLETC in February, I worked hard. I thanked my lucky stars I wasn't going in the summer. The heat and humidity have downed many a student. They even had non-physical exertion days for the safety of the summer students. February was just fine and, back then, training was only eleven weeks long. I packed up my van named Killarney and started my drive east from Arizona. I had built in some extra days to sightsee along the way. I definitely wanted to go through Texas to see the McDonald Observatory at Fort Davis. Astronomy is one of my hobbies, and "Star Date" on the radio was a favorite broadcast of mine. My second day on the road saw me east of El Paso and I turned onto Route 166 South toward Fort Davis, stopping to see a great sunset. I thought the air smelled like sulfur and was glad I didn't live there. As I drove on, there was a popping sound from the engine and more of a sulfur smell, then the headlights went out and the engine died, as I coasted to a stop on the side of the road. It was dusk as I got out and looked up and down the road. I tried 911 on my cell phone. It was one of those suitcase phones that had a complete handset! But there was no service. Then I saw a car and flagged it down. It was a General Services Administration (GSA) vehicle, and so I knew the driver was a government employee. It was Ramon, who worked for the NPS as the Chief of Mexico Affairs. What a great guy. He used his cell phone to call his dad who called a wrecker in Fort Davis. Ramon insisted on staying until the tow truck came. Jimmy, the truck operator, brought us into town to a local motel and returned in the morning to take Killarney to his shop for repair.

The next day I toured Fort Davis while Jimmy worked on Killarney. It turned out my electrical systems were "toast." All of my lights, my battery and, worst of all, my computer processor were fried. The nearest repair parts were in Odessa, Texas, 150 miles away. Jimmy and I left at 4:45 a.m. to make the trip to the repair shop with Killarney in tow. The moon was a sliver with Jupiter in the night sky, and the constellations were brilliant. The McDonald Observatory would have to wait for another time. Jimmy delivered me to Dwayne at the Odessa dealership. I rented a room a short distance away and napped, as I hadn't slept well the previous night. I tell you, Odessa may be bleak in appearance at first glance, with the oilrigs and open vastness, but the people were golden. I received such kind support and thoughtfulness. After 6:00 p.m., Dwayne had replaced the computer processor, voltage regulator, alternator and bulbs Jimmy didn't have and she started up. Thank goodness! I was poorer, but on the road. I drove over 1,000 miles in 24 hours, stopping in rest stops along the way. But I had a heck of a time finding a room in New Orleans ... it turned out I arrived during Mardi Gras! So I kept driving east. During the trip, I tried to run every day, even in parking lots, to keep my edge for the PEB. I arrived at the Guard Entrance Station at FLETC with two hours to spare. I checked in my issued Sig Sauer 9mm pistol and went to registration. There I began to meet my classmates.

The course was the Land Management Training Program. (Now it's called Land Management Police Training.) It was not wholly composed of NPS staff. There were folks from the U.S. Forest Service, Department of Defense, Tennessee Valley Authority, U.S. Bureau of Land Management, and the U.S. Fish and Wildlife Service. When we registered, we received our identification cards that affiliated us with the Department of the Treasury. I was assigned to a dorm that was more than a mile from the classroom and shared a bathroom with a female U.S. Customs Agent from New York. It was cozy and soon became home. The dining facilities were incredible. They served thousands of meals a day with good choices and variety. The salad bars were awesome.

Our check-in day included assigned clothes: dark blue pants and lighter blue shirts. We called ourselves "Smurfs." Then, in the physical training (PT) section we were issued everything, including shirts, shorts, bras, socks, swimsuits and jockstraps (as needed). If it wasn't issued, we didn't wear it! We turned it in after each use to be issued clean "used" clothes in return. We worked out daily and our first challenge was the PEB. The track was a million-dollar track, we were told. It was spongy and comfortable. I ran like the wind at sea level, taking minutes off of my time from 7,000 feet at the rim of the canyon. It also included a body fat measurement, weighted bench press, agility run, and trunk flexibility test. We cheered each other on and formed a nice class bond. We eventually formed a softball team and had great competitions with the other agencies on campus. I did well, passing the PEB, as did all of my classmates. Our PT each day varied from gym work, defensive tactics, weight work, circuit training and our very favorite – note the sarcasm here – group run. It was just like the military. We were lined in formation and jogged down the road together. An instructor taught us all kinds of things to sing out as we ran.

Instructor: "My old grandma's ninety-three!"

Students: "My old grandma's ninety-three!"

Instructor: "She likes PT just like me!"

Students: "She likes PT just like me!"

We never sang expletives, at least not loud enough for the instructors to hear.

After I studied every night, I would go out to enjoy the fireflies. There were tons of notes, handouts, tests and lectures. We were tested over and over, placed in scenarios, and did building searches, car stops and mock trials in a courtroom. We learned photography, interview techniques and how to lift fingerprints with a multitude of devices and chemistries. Our instructors included Assistant U.S. District Attorneys, university professors, and experienced officers from all agencies. The lectures on Criminal Law were especially excellent and entertaining with Gil as the lead instructor. We went to behavioral lab and had interviews taped for later review. We learned non-lethal compliance and arrest techniques, and had a lot of time on the firing range. There were both indoor and outdoor ranges, as well as scenario situations where we used non-functional red-handled pistols. We also went full-out in defensive tactics when we had "redman" practice. Students would dress in red-colored, full-body padded suits and we would have at it with batons and collapsible batons. We continued our daily PT and we were all getting into great shape. My defense tactics partner was Lindy. She was smaller than I but could really swing a baton. We would yell and order each other in the scenarios and whack each other with rubber batons trying to hit the padded guard we held. We often missed and were black and blue by the end of the day. You could hear us order each other down as in an arrest and then, *sotto voce*, "Sorry, sorry," as we realized we'd whacked the other on her real leg or arm.

On the weekends I left. I drove to Savannah, went to a Dodger baseball game at Vero Beach, canoed 21 miles of the Altamaha River with five classmates, snorkeled with manatees at Crystal Springs, did a SCUBA dive at Homasassa Springs, went to the Kennedy Space Center and more. Early on, I went to a Georgia Welcome Center and read about what to see and do. On the bulletin board was a creased paper that invited all to attend the Baptist Church in Plains, Georgia, and to meet President Jimmy Carter on Sundays. I thought it was interesting, but it never occurred to me it was authentic. If it was, why drive all that way to see him from one hundred feet away? I read about and later visited the park areas at Fort Fredericka, Fort Augustine, Fort Pulaski, Fort Sumter . . . I see a pattern here.

Our driving course work was a mix of lectures and "hands on." We were paired up and had radio contact with instructors who corrected us over the radio as we drove the course. It was a big track and we chased other cars in pursuit driving training. My partner was Laurence and we hit it off well. We were different in our techniques and soon earned the nicknames, Chaos and Calm. I was Calm, which was fairly interesting as Laurence (Chaos) was a quiet unassuming guy, until you got him behind the wheel of a car. Yikes! We never rolled, but came close a few times. He cackled with glee on the straight-aways and made screeching car noises when we went around curves. Thank goodness we wore helmets! When it came to our driving tests, we were all a bit nervous. If you failed, you had to "remediate" and that would make you ineligible for performance awards at graduation. It was finally my turn for the emergency pursuit driving test. With our helmets on, I drove while Laurence sat in the passenger seat. We had to talk on the radio and drive at the same time. We had to take curves without driving out of bounds and complete the course under a specified time. We practiced and practiced, coached each other and then it was the real deal.

There was one curve in particular that was a tight corner, and it was easy to fishtail or take it too slow and not make the time. As I approached, I knew I had nailed it and came out of it perfectly. I was so pleased that I almost rolled the car on the next easy curve! I locked the brakes, skidded and fishtailed leaving a plume of tire smoke in my wake. But I recovered and thankfully completed the course cleanly and on time. Of course, my classmates asked me what I was barbecuing on the course, once they learned I had passed and could kid me unmercifully.

Laurence was also my partner when we had to experience pepper spray first hand. Oleoresin capsaicin (OC) has replaced chemical mace as the preferred non-lethal aerosol used to subdue suspects. And we were required to experience it first hand. This was, in part, so that if we were accidentally exposed to it in the field, we knew what we were getting into. It also let us realize we would survive such an exposure. When the instructor sprayed me, he got me full in my face. My eyes glued shut, they burned and I teared terribly. But I made it and Laurence helped spray my face with water and brought me towels. We all took care of each other.

Part way through the class, my husband Kent was able to fly out for a weekend visit. It was great to see him and we escaped to

Amelia Island. At home, I am a light sleeper and he is a heavy sleeper. He told me that after I left, our Golden Retriever Shannon jumped up on the bed and slept all night, and Kent never realized this until the next morning.

By the time our weekend together ended, I was ready for the second half of training. It was more hands-on with building searches, paintball "active" shootouts, and shoot/don't-shoot scenarios. We interviewed people in the field and ran after "suspects."

Toward the end, we received a lot of specialty training. It included marijuana eradication, recognizing different weapons and how to disable them, (pre-911) terrorism training, and motorcycle groups and gangs. We pulled it all together with all day and night scenarios. We began with a call to a house or accident scene. We did investigations and decided if lawful infractions had occurred. We wrote criminal complaints and took them to a pretend judge to authorize them, then served warrants ... sometimes not peacefully. We did stakeouts in the evening rain and conducted felony stops on dirt roads. We testified in mock trials in court. It was a good way to bring it all together. When graduation day came we were all so very proud and, quite frankly, glad it was over. We were ready to go home. Kent flew out for graduation and we drove back to Arizona together. But two weeks before graduation, I had one more trip to make on a weekend.

I drove to Americus, Georgia, and then on to Plains. The Jimmy Carter Museum was still in the depot house, but my focus was the Maranatha Baptist Church. At 9:00 a.m., I followed about fifty people into the pews while a minister gave a short sermon. Then, in came President Jimmy Carter and Rosalynn with the Secret Service. They sat right in front of me. President Carter stood and gave a thirty-minute talk on their latest humanitarian endeavors. It was all being recorded as living history. There was a break and I walked among the pecan trees to the beautiful singing of the cardinals and mockingbirds. The air got a bit humid and heavy by noon when the rest of the service was over. The Carters invited all to meet them and I did. I walked right up and introduced myself. They were genuinely happy to meet me and raved about the Grand Canyon; Rosalynn noted it was one of her favorite parks. I was fortunate to get a photo and a lasting memory. FLETC allowed me the opportunity to grow and become a professional in my career. It also afforded me an opportunity as a citizen of the United States, to meet one of the country's leaders; a leader who stepped down in a peaceful exchange of government and then became a true worldwide humanitarian.

WASHING MY HAIR

As a seasonal naturalist early in my career at Lodgepole in Sequoia National Park, I had the best of two worlds. I got to give nature walks and talks, and to help out on the occasional medical call as a paramedic. A disturbing pattern was beginning to emerge, though. By some very strange coincidence, many times when I washed my hair, a medical call would come in. Even if I thought about it, a call would come. It got to the point where the Protection Rangers would ask whether I planned to wash my hair on particular evenings so they could plan around the inevitable call. It was silly fun, but a perplexing coincidence.

One morning on my late-schedule day, I had a great run to Tokopah Falls and back, and jumped into the shower, yes, to wash my hair. Only three feet to a side, the shower stall was made of metal. If you touched a wall on a cold morning you could get frostbite in a hot shower! Its entrance had a simple shower curtain.

Unbeknownst to me, as I enjoyed my shower, a three-year-old ventured inside a tent at the campground and got into his grandmother's overnight case. His parents found him with a partially empty bottle of Valium in his hands, the top off, pills in his mouth and pills on the tent floor. The panicked family rushed the little boy to the Visitor Center for help. The Protection Ranger/EMT realized this could be life-threatening with a two-hour drive to the nearest hospital. He sent Steve, a member of the wildland fire brigade, to find me. His first stop was my rented government cabin up on a hill.

Steve raced up the drive and to the door. He later said he

pounded on the door, but I never heard him. I only knew that in one instant, the shower curtain was torn to the side and a frantic Steve said, "Nancy, a baby has overdosed on Valium and they need you right away."

I said, "Okay Steve, I'll be right there."

Steve then added, as if I were dressed and in any normal room, "Can I get anything for you?"

"Sure, Steve," I said, "grab my medic bag and I'll be right out."

He ran out of the tiny bathroom and I followed him within a minute, in my jumpsuit and wet hair. We drove to the Visitor Center and as I walked in, the Rangers stared at my wet hair with knowing glances. Sigh.

I quickly assessed the child who had good vital signs. I called the Base Station Physician and we agreed on a plan: activated charcoal by mouth for the child, and a calm but immediate trip to the ER. I am happy to report our treatment was successful and the toddler did fine.

But the most disturbing part of the call was when I talked to Steve afterwards about his grand entrance into my bathroom. He shrugged and apologized, admitting to being a little "amped up." Most disturbing was his tunnel vision; at least, I hope that is what it was. He said he never remembered seeing me naked in the shower! I was still single then, and it was not a great compliment to my ego. However, they did install a phone in my cabin so they could call me out, and I could call them with a warning when I was going to wash my hair. ❑

Jumpers

Rarely a day went by when a visitor didn't ask the inevitable question, "How many people die by falling off the edge of the canyon?"

Many asked out of nervousness while at Mather Point, a major visitor overlook with railings and fencing. The straight-down view was dizzying. Some asked out of morbid curiosity. I finally learned to tell most that in a given year, anywhere from three to a dozen folks could die at the canyon, but rarely from a fall from the rim. Many had pre-existing medical problems that were aggravated by the lower oxygen content at the 7,000-foot elevation of the South Rim ... and the North Rim was almost 1,500 feet higher in spots. Some died in motor vehicle collisions. But falls from the rim did happen, some accidentally and some purposely. One August was a nightmare!

Just after 4:00 p.m., a visitor to the park named David was walking along the rim about 200 yards west of Mather Point. David saw a man crouched under a tree about fifteen feet from the edge. He walked past the man and noted the man never looked up at him, just stared toward the rim. After he passed the man, he turned around out of curiosity and saw the man run to the edge and jump. The man never screamed or uttered a sound. David was stunned as he ran to the edge. There was a thirty-foot drop, then a slope of about one hundred feet. The man was crumpled up, his white t-shirt and blue jeans stained with red about 150 feet below the rim.

David then heard the man moan and cry out, "God, why are you punishing me? Please help me. Can anyone hear me? Someone, please help me!"

David went toward Mather Point and found a couple with a cell phone. They dialed 911 and Ranger Kent was on scene in minutes, taking IC (Incident Command) with other Rangers en route. Ranger Parkmedic Matt was next on scene and set up for a hasty rappel to the victim. Ranger Rosie arrived and was given investigations, then Ranger Ivan, who was given on-scene operations. I arrived next and quickly locked my defensive gear, including my gun and body armor in the trunk of my patrol sedan and pulled out my Search and Rescue (SAR) bag. I arrived as yellow police tape was being strung through the trees to keep folks out of the staging area. Kent and Ivan asked me to rappel down to help Matt with the victim. The jumper's name was Christopher and he was 31 years old. He had difficulty breathing with chest pain, fluid in his lung, an avulsed foot and multiple fractures. We would prepare for a shorthaul once the patient was packaged.

I walked to the side of the staging area and dug into my SAR bag. I pulled out my seat harness that had many things already attached, dangling from the belt. I stepped through and fastened the buckle, making sure I doubled it back. I had my webbing, extra carabiners, pre-tied prussic lines, ascenders, figure-eight, rappel rack, shorthaul lines, emergency knife and gloves. My gloves didn't have fingers so I could protect my palms but still have the dexterity of my fingers as needed. I slipped on my chest harness and secured it, then my climbing helmet. I went to the belay station where I was double-checked for all the correct equipment and that all was safely secured. There I received a safety briefing. I was handed the end of the belay line and tied a figure-eight knot with a long tail. I passed the tail through my seat harness attachment, then followed through the original figure eight with another, securing it with a following knot.

I passed the rappel rope through my figure-eight hardware rather than my rappel rack. I would be stepping down most of the time rather than free rappelling. This was a faster method for me.

"On belay," I called.

"On belay," came the reply.

"On rappel," I called.

"Rappel on," came the reply.

I stepped to the edge of the canyon and began to descend, off to one side of the rescue scene. I didn't want to be directly over Matt and Christopher and shower rocks down upon them. Matt had taken an extra helmet and webbing with him and secured Christopher on his arrival. I looked up and signaled I was ready for the equipment. Already having an oxygen cylinder and medical bag on my back, I now reached up for a backboard and Bauman bag tied to another belay rope that I would work down to the scene.

This area west of Mather Point was not a straight shot down. There was some free air for about thirty feet that I rappelled, but after that there was a slope of about forty degrees with limestone rocks, bushes, pinyon pine and juniper trees. In some places it was so dense, you could not easily see out to the canyon. I listened as the radio in my chest harness crackled with logistics conversations. It didn't take long before I arrived just above and to the east of Matt and Christopher. There wasn't much room to maneuver.

"Hey Matt," I called.

"Hey," he replied.

Matt was in great shape but I could see he was hot and strained from the effort of trying to hold Christopher in a manner that would protect his neck and spinal column as well as keep him somewhat immobile on the slope. Christopher was crying and anxious.

He repeatedly said, "Save me. I don't want to die."

Matt and I took turns reassuring him we would take good care of him.

I asked Matt what he wanted me to do, as I worked my way over to them with the equipment. He had already started an IV line and we discussed packaging him for shorthaul. I put him on oxygen by nasal cannula and heard Matt's assessment of his injuries. As Matt stated the litany of fractures, contusions and pains he'd found, I thought silently to myself that it would have been easier to tell me what wasn't busted. While Christopher's ankle was at a horribly bent angle with bones protruding, it wasn't as life-threatening as the surely collapsed lung and the bleeding in his chest cavity that Matt and I suspected. Matt wondered about pain medicine, but when we measured Christopher's blood pressure, it was below 100 points systolic, and we knew that morphine would be too dangerous. As a narcotic, it could further decrease his pressure as it dilated his blood vessels, sending him further into shock. We tried to open the IV to give him more fluid, but it was tough with the IV fluid bag lying above him on the rocky slope.

We placed a cervical collar around Christopher's neck and I went to the foot end of the backboard. I slipped the backboard under him as best as I could while Matt held him carefully. Then I reached up and held his shoulders and neck from below while Matt pulled the rest of the board under him. We slid on the dry slope and I couldn't help thinking about my water bottle I had inadvertently left with my pack on the rim. I held the board up from the foot end to keep Christopher as level as possible. I locked my arms into my chest under my chin and crouched in a tight roll so my body would take the weight more than my arms. Matt began securing Christopher with webbing, letting other parts of the patient's own body splint injured areas. By tying his legs together and his arms to his sides, his multiple fractured areas would, at least, not move around too much. We made no effort to reduce the angulated and open ankle fracture, it just hung out there. Matt relieved me while I pulled out the Bauman bag. It was a large red canvas-like sack that went around the patient and backboard. We took turns enveloping Christopher into the bag, and I again held the board as level as possible.

Matt then prepared for shorthaul: getting his lines ready, securing the harness and completing communications with the Operations Ranger. We slid the packaged Christopher further down slope and to the side to a more open spot. There was a single untied line through a loop of the bag I would hold to keep them from swinging as they lifted off. It also served to keep Christopher from sliding into the canyon should either Matt or

I lose our grip on him. But once the helicopter arrived, the rope could not be secured to the ground because it would have the unwanted effect of securing the helicopter to the ground once it hooked onto the patient and rescuer.

Matt marshaled the chopper in and the lift line was lowered perfectly. Matt clipped the bag and himself onto the golden ring and gave the signal to go up. I paid out the line until it slipped free of the bag and they were airborne. Matt and Christopher rose into the blue sky, just minutes away from the parking lot at Canyon View Plaza. There the patient was transferred to Guardian Ambulance, which took him to the NPS helibase where he was flown to Flagstaff Medical Center. The Incident Commander later called the attending physician and was assured that his concerns about Christopher's attempted suicide would be addressed. He told the IC Christopher was in surgery for all the fractures and internal injuries. We later learned he lived and was in therapy.

In the interim, I picked up the scene of cut garments, shoes, medical trash and leftover webbing. I put them in my pack and communicated to the Operations Ranger I was ready to ascend. They had the hand crank, mechanical advantage raise system set up, and I walked up easily with the top rescuers doing most of the work. I arrived on top, weary but mostly thirsty. I downed a quart of water in one swoop and looked for more. We cleaned up and had a debriefing. What a day.

* * * *

Unbelievably, not two weeks later, we received a call of a possible jumper to the west of Mather Point. I felt a major déjà vu and wondered if it wasn't some sort of a sick joke. I arrived first on scene and went just a bit to the east of where Christopher had jumped. Ranger Mike quickly joined me as we heard moaning and groaning about 120 to 150 feet down. I took Incident Command this time and Mike went down to assess the situation. The slope was not as steep and Mike traversed to just above the patient. I could hear Mike talk to an agitated male, and then there was yelling. Mike called up to me on the local radio channel. He said there was a male in his late twenties who was upset and agitated and injured. But this time, the jumper did not want help. He cussed out Mike and threatened to take him with him if he could only stand to jump the rest of the way. Mike prudently stayed above and to the side of the jumper and tried to calm him down. We soon had an army of SAR Rangers. The jumper was restrained physically and chemically, and pulled up to the rim where he, too, received medical and psychiatric help at Flagstaff Medical Center. In our debriefing later, we began to joke about handing out a map for potential jumpers with arrows that said, "Jump here, not here." These two jumpers didn't go directly off from Mather Point where certain death would find them hundreds of feet below the sheer cliffs. While it was crude black humor, we kept it to ourselves and it helped to release our stress.

* * * *

Then there was John. John was a vagrant who managed to elude us Rangers for weeks. We would receive reports of him over the railing at Mather Point, picking up the coins visitors threw onto the distant flat areas as if they were making a wish. John would then go buy liquor and, on occasion, he would be arrested for disorderly conduct. But he always managed to make it back to the canyon from the jail. It was only later that we learned he lived in a small cave below the rim near Mather Point.

Just after noon on September 2, John was again over the railing picking up coins. Many visitors called to him telling him it was dangerous and that he should come back. John just laughed at them and continued to stagger over the rock surfaces. It was apparent to many that he was intoxicated. Someone went to get a cell phone as John began to play to the crowd.

He finally yelled, "Watch me fly!"

Then he jumped toward a pinnacle that was easily fifteen feet away. Scores of visitors watched in horror as this 51-year-old male fell into the abyss below Mather Point. Ranger Donnie was first on scene just minutes after the call came into Park Dispatch. He stood at the top of the stairs and ordered everyone to stay put. He had all the witnesses corralled onto the overlook and was able to garner excellent eyewitness accounts and subsequent written statements before onlookers could disperse. Rangers Kent and Tammy arrived and Kent took Operations as Donnie continued Incident Command and Investigations. Patty, Chuck and I arrived soon after. Although we knew the probable outcome, Tammy set up for a hasty rappel from the railing at Mather Point. We belayed her over the edge and, at about 150 feet straight down, she hit dirt and rocks and blood and body parts. It was apparent that John had continued on quite a ways and Tammy returned to the rim. Patty, Chuck and I donned our SAR gear. With Tammy we went to the west of Mather Point to a little-known animal trail and began the long traverse down.

We started at the 7,150-foot elevation on the rim and climbed down to the slope below the cliffs of Mather Point at about 6,830 feet. We then hiked east. We could see where John had impacted the canyon; from there we determined the rest of the fall line. At 6,790 feet, we found most of him at his final resting place. We were each given specific assignments in the on-scene investigation once we determined John had not survived. There were many tasks that had to be accomplished: photography, death investigation, sketch of the fall line, on-scene safety and others. Our first task was to be safe; then to try to find all of John. He was 117 feet from the base of the cliff with his head downhill. His right shoe was missing, his clothes were torn to shreds and it was apparent on our cursory exam he had multiple fractures. I completed the head-to-toe assessment with gloves on and sensed crepitus, the grinding of broken bones, over his skull, facial bones, torso, sternum, ribs, pelvis and all extremities. I then volunteered to draw the fall line. This involved drawing a map of the fall, the final resting place and body position and one other component. From the body, multiple rays were drawn inches, feet, and sometimes scores of feet from the deceased. These lines identified body parts that were no longer attached to the deceased. But my most amazing find has puzzled me for years. As we located all of John, about five feet away on a flat rock there was a perfectly round eyeball. The brown iris was straight up and the pupil still discernable. Two inches away from the eyeball, on the same rock, was a small, pearly white sack. I suddenly realized it was a perfectly preserved testicle that had been torn from the scrotum and somehow landed right next to the avulsed eyeball. Everyone came over and just stared at the pair for a few moments. No one said a thing, though Chuck may have cringed a bit. The photos were taken, and the two wayward body parts were bagged and tagged as I continued my search for John's body parts to complete my drawing. We were down below the rim for

Plains – *Tyrolean traverse on the Russian River, California.*

Right: *River short haul rescue of stranded boat passengers, Grand Canyon National Park.*

Below: Bounty Hunters – *Teaching rappelling to Explorer Scout Jacob, Grand Canyon National Park.*

First Flight – *Nancy and Pilot Jerry, Grand Canyon National Park.*

Jumpers – *901 recovery team: Tammy, Patty, Nancy and Chuck, Grand Canyon National Park.*

Preparations for horse patrol,
Grand Canyon National Park.
Photo: Sean Brady

Helping a visitor with directions.
Photo: Sean Brady.

Left & Below: **Pima Point** – *Pima Point 901 recovery, Grand Canyon National Park.*

Heart Park –
*Living history character,
Shelley Simmons, Sequoia
National Park.*

Ranger naturalist children's walk, Sequoia National Park.

Working with the community children, Grand Canyon National Park.

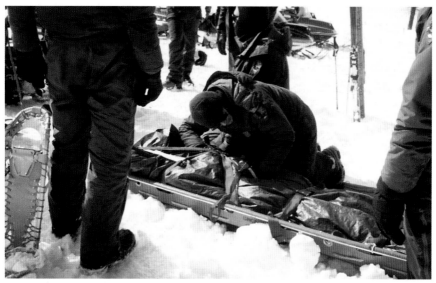

Winter search and rescue training, northern Arizona.

Right: *As a Wildland Fire Medical Unit Leader exploring an old tree-based fire lookout tower, North Rim of the Grand Canyon.*

Below: *Structural Fire Captain on vertical ventilation training, Grand Canyon National Park.*

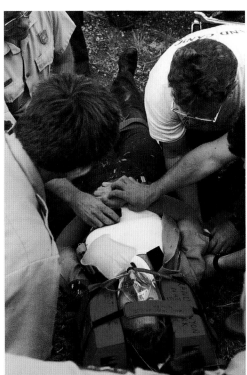

Personal Injury – *Full spinal precautions, Grand Canyon National Park.*

Plains – *With President Jimmy and Rosalynn Carter, Plains, Georgia.*

Search and rescue training, Grand Canyon National Park.

Exploring fossils as a Naturalist Ranger, Death Valley National Park.

Resource management duties at a packrat midden, Grand Canyon National Park.

Stabilizing a patient with a head injury, Grand Canyon National Park.

Structural Fire Brigade member, Sequoia National Park.

Heart Park – *Completing the John Muir and High Sierra Trails, California.*

about two hours when we received word from the coroner that we had permission to move the body. The park helicopter brought a body bag in a net on a long line and lowered it to us. We placed all of John in the body bag and loaded it in the net for the chopper's return. We soon had the net clipped onto the long-line and then the four of us were alone. We had our own quiet debriefing, looked out over the canyon and began our climb back up to the rim.

911

It was my Friday so I had the early shift. On duty, I drove down to the horse corral at 6:00 a.m. to feed the gang. I flaked off hay according to the number of head in the corral; this day there were only two. I put the hay in the wheelbarrow and rolled it over to their food troughs. With a pitchfork, I carefully lifted the hay into the different feeding areas. I was careful because there is nothing worse than getting even one piece of hay down your shirt, between you and your body armor. I had to place the hay in separate troughs, or else the dominant horse would bite and kick the other away and he'd go hungry. Then I filled up the water trough. I was enjoying the crisp early morning when Dispatch called. They had received a 911 call with no one at the other end. This happens especially when kids were playing around, but then she gave me the address and I realized the call could be serious.

The address, about one mile away, was of a friend and long-time resident who had been in the community for years. I also knew he had a heart condition because the previous year I had flown him to the hospital when he had chest pains and suffered a myocardial infarction.

I sped silently to the home – no need to wake up the world this early with sirens. There was no traffic and I was at the residence in minutes. I went to the doorway and knocked. No answer. I rang the doorbell and, again, no answer. I called out "Hello," and my friend's name. I was really getting worried now. I wasn't sure if his wife was home, but no one was answering me. I radioed to Dispatch that I was entering the residence.

I turned the doorknob and it was unlocked. The house was eerily quiet as I walked into the hallway. Again I called out, identified myself and asked if all was okay. I took two more steps and there he was.

With a big smile on his face and fastening the belt on his trousers, he sauntered leisurely down the hall as if it was not at all unusual to have an armed paramedic standing in this hallway at 6:15 in the morning.

"Are you okay?" I asked.

"Sure," he said, "I'm fine. What's up?"

I explained the 911 call that Dispatch had traced back to his home.

"Really?" he replied. "I didn't call," he said with a perplexed look on his face.

I stayed in the hall as he walked back to his bedroom and then came right back, assuring me the phone was on the hook.

He then went into the den and, with a smile, poked his head back out and said, "Look at this."

I walked into the den with him and there, curled around the phone, was the family cat. The phone line was open on the desk. We laughed at the realization that the cat had accidentally hit the speed dial 911 button then curled up to wait for the festivities. I also laughed in relief. ❏

Firefighter Down

The call was for a dumpster fire near Trailer Village on the South Rim of the Grand Canyon. It was a cold November night, so my husband Kent, the park's Structural Fire Chief, and I responded. I was a firefighter and engineer at the time. We met a third firefighter, Jude, at the station. We jumped into our turnouts and Kent drove us to the smoldering dumpster, about a mile away. He would be the Engineer and Jude and I would douse the fire.

For the most part, dumpster fires are urgent calls that let you use your firefighter skills without too much of a threat to life and limb. Although it may seem benign, there are plenty of things in dumpsters that can harm and kill. Wool, for instance, gives off cyanide gas when it burns, and more than once we have found butane cylinders improperly disposed of in a dumpster. They are just like bombs when they explode, sending harmful shrapnel in all directions. We were sure to take the proper precautions.

We pulled up beyond the dumpster, and Kent activated the pump and chocked the engine while Jude and I did buddy checks on our Self-Contained Breathing Apparatus (SCBA) tanks, turnouts and helmet. We had a fifty-foot pre-connect with an automatic nozzle for just this situation, and connected the 1-inch hose to the discharge of the pump. I took the nozzle and Jude the roof hook. We approached the dumpster with caution as Kent turned a strong halogen light on our work location. I signaled for water with a moving arc of my arm over my head and Kent charged the line. It snapped into a straight line and became heavy but manageable. While crouched down, Jude used the roof hook to open the lid of the dumpster a small distance. When nothing horrible came out of the dumpster, he opened it about forty-five degrees and held the handle with the hook. Smoke continued to puff out, but it was fairly light. I opened the nozzle slowly to prevent a pressure wave from hammering the pump and sprayed the inside of the lid so the water rained down into the dumpster. Then we stood and flooded the partially-filled dumpster. We pulled out plastic garbage bags, ripped and sprayed them, and stirred things up thoroughly until we were sure the last of the charcoal briquettes that started the fire were extinguished. Sigh. It always makes me wonder why people think they can put hot coals in a bin of trash, despite signs and common sense. I wonder why they call it common sense when it's not that common.

We put the soaked trash back in the dumpster and took our SCBAs off and replaced the cylinders. Kent had returned to the cab and had put the engine in neutral to shut the pump down when Dispatch came over the radio with an alert tone:

"Report of a fully involved trailer fire in Tusayan next to the Stix Market; possible occupants still inside."

Kent immediately ordered a General Alarm to call all available firefighters. At that time, the town of Tusayan did not have a fire department. The National Park Service responded to help the town on a mutual aid basis for all emergencies, including structural fires. Kent ordered Jude to bring the telescoped halogen light into place and for me to disconnect the fifty-foot quick attack hose from the pump. I had no time to roll it up so I took the nozzle off and threw the hose in the bushes. We would return to get it later and it wouldn't be missed with all the other hose the engine carried.

I jumped into the Captain's seat and Jude jumped into the back of the engine. We fastened our seatbelts and Kent drove us Code 3, with lights and sirens, down South Entrance Road and out of the park. It was a five-mile drive from Camper Services to the entrance and less than one mile from there to the market. As we got closer, I began to see a glow in the night sky reflecting off the low clouds. When we passed the Forest Service work area, I gasped as I could see a wall of flames shooting into the night sky higher than the IMAX Theater! I immediately said to myself, "This is the real deal; this is no dumpster fire." My mouth got dry and I truly got a bit scared. That got worse when Kent pulled up in front of the IMAX and stopped. He turned the engine over to me and said he would run ahead to give a scene size-up. He didn't want to bring the engine closer because he was sure the only thing that could make flames jump scores of feet into the air was a propane tank on fire and he didn't want us to drive into a BLEVE (Boiling, Liquid, Expanding, Vapor, Explosion.) Some BLEVEs have caused railroad tank cars of propane to be launched and land over a mile away. As I exited the engine to run around to the driver's side, I called to Kent to be careful as I saw him run toward the inferno. Boy, was I ever scared for him. But then I knew he was the best at his craft and would be careful. I just hoped the fire knew that, too.

Within a minute, Kent called a report into Dispatch and ordered the engine into place to catch a hydrant and park safely for the attack. As I came over the hill and past the IMAX, I could see an eighty-foot trailer parked adjacent to the north wall of the Stix Market. It was about eight feet away from the wall. Between the trailer and the market was a large, industrial propane tank that was emitting flames high into the air. The trailer was on fire and the wall of the market was a threatened exposure. I knew from training that it was better to have a propane tank off-gassing with the emission on fire than to have one totally sealed and being cooked to BLEVE point. It was the lesser of two evils, but it was intimidating. Then the entire relief valve assembly blew off the propane tank, releasing fire and propane even higher into the air with a loud explosion.

Kent relayed assignments to us after we caught the hydrant. I put on my SCBA as Jude, also an Engineer, took over the pump. Airport firefighters, concession firefighters and Engine 2 from Grand Canyon all showed up. An open hose line was placed on the fully involved trailer. Another open line was placed on the exposure, the wall to the market. When Engine 2 arrived, it parked on the backside of the market and hit the propane tank with an open, charged line to cool it down. A closed hose line was extended into the market. It was charged, but the nozzle stayed shut as firefighters stood by in case the fire breached the wall of the market.

I was on the nozzle on the trailer. I was crouched down under the chassis directing the water at the fire source. It quickly began to get smaller. I couldn't do more until more firefighters arrived, and so I laid on the hose and periodically opened the nozzle to keep the fire at bay. When additional firefighters came, we were able to advance the line and go between the market and trailer to put out the fire. Within minutes the propane tank fire had been extinguished and the cooling measures continued. The backside firefighters entered the part of the trailer that was not destroyed and radioed that the occupant had escaped unharmed. Happy days. Behind me, advancing the hose was Paul. I had worked with him for years and he was a good guy. Things were calming down, but not over. Then the backside engine said their tank was almost empty and that they still needed to secure a water source. They were attempting to connect to a hydrant. Kent ordered our line to advance to the rear until the backside regained water. I was on the nozzle and the two hundred feet of charged hose was heavy. Paul was behind me with another firefighter as we worked hard to haul the closed line forward. There was water everywhere, dripping from the trailer, the propane tank and the market wall, making huge puddles. I pulled hard on the line just as Paul turned his back to me and began to haul hose in earnest. I stepped into a puddle and was gone.

I had fallen into a huge water-filled cavern and could not feel the bottom. I was fully submerged and, with Paul's back to me feeding me hoseline, I was being pushed ever deeper. I had been a SCUBA diver for years, but this was really different. It was inky black in the cavern, some sort of basement lift access. I could still breathe because of my SCBA, but I couldn't get out, couldn't feel the bottom, and hung onto the hose like a lifeline, which it was. I called out into my mask, "Help, help!" but no one heard.

At the moment I fell, Kent had turned in our direction and watched as I plummeted out of sight. It was like a magician's trick. One second I was there and the next I was not.

He immediately called on the radio, "Firefighter down, market wall!"

When you hear that call, all firefighting stops and the efforts are solely geared to saving the firefighter. I didn't hear any of this, but Paul did and turned around to see the hose bend down into the depths of the bottomless pit of water. With almost superhuman strength, Paul single-handedly pulled the charged line and one waterlogged firefighter out of the depths of the hole. I landed like a fish on my belly on the concrete beside the hole and then, before I could even try to stand, I was being carried away from the fire to the staging area. I pulled off my SCBA mask and looked around at a lot of eyes.

I smiled and said, "Wow, that was something . . . I thought it was only a puddle!"

I could hear the relief in everyone's exhalation, including Kent who was peering over the shoulders of the firefighters who had pulled me out. Paul was apologizing profusely and we laughed as he helped me out of my SCBA backpack. The incident medic was there and asked if I was okay. I said, yes, that I was just waterlogged. I took off my turnout coat and went to the front of the engine. I did a handstand, propping my feet against the hood and water poured out of my rubber boots and bunker pants. When I came to my feet, I realized just how cold the November night was and put some blankets over my shoulders as I took a break at the rehabilitation area.

Once I warmed up, I took my cup of hot cocoa and watched my fellow firefighters begin the mop-up. The fire was out and no one was injured, not even me. Mike, a Ranger who was working security, came over to see how I was. We chuckled at the weird events of my dunking and he told me that, at the height of the fire suppression, somehow an intoxicated man was able to get through the security line. The inebriated fellow stepped over the hoselines and past firefighters until he entered the market. The clerk had been evacuated so the drunk went up to the firefighters on standby with the charged line and asked them to sell him some liquor! Mike soon had him in custody. What a night.

MY DAM ASSIGNMENT

Since that horrible day of September 11, 2001, safety and security in America has changed forever. Many of the changes were obvious, and some were truly subtle. But they weren't subtle to Park Rangers who had a Law Enforcement Commission. We already carried semiautomatic handguns; mine was a Sig Sauer 9mm. We were proficient with shotguns and M16 rifles. Now, post-911, as Federal Law Enforcement Officers, we were subject to Homeland Security assignments. There just weren't enough Federal Officers around. It's not just training, but also the evaluation and background checks that could take up to six months for each position.

Rangers in Grand Canyon and other parks were assigned to off-park assignments, and those left behind had to pick up the slack. We worked extra hours and on our lieu days. It was tiring after awhile, but there were no other alternatives at the time. I used to say I'd be rich from the overtime, but I'd be dead from the exhaustion.

It was my turn in July to go out of park to a Homeland Security assignment. It was located at a western dam in the desert. We were in two teams with three to a team and a team leader. We were split into dayshift and nightshift. I was out on the dayshift. We started at 6:00 a.m. and finished at 7:00 p.m., if we were lucky. We worked 21 days straight. Our duties varied but they were mostly confined and strict, intending for us to be a visual presence. In one area we checked buses all day. All the passengers would exit and we would look inside, underneath (with mirrors), and in the cargo compartments. We were looking for weapons and explosives. We gave a nice talk prior to getting the passengers off and, before they got back on, we got them in line and checked each one's satchel or bag and eyeballed them for weapons. Remember, this was in July and although the bus passengers were only offloaded for a short time, we were in the sun a lot. It was dehydrating, and I went through water like crazy. My body armor felt twice as heavy by the end of shift.

Another station checked the dam workers in and out of the dam itself. We checked their identifications (IDs) and noted license plates. Then we would be assigned a place on the road near the dam to be a presence. It's not why I became a Park Ranger, but the world had changed and so did I.

One morning I was assigned the lead at the Visitor Center complex. I was actually able to get out of my car and walk around the grounds and the above ground area, just being a presence. We all had received an orientation prior to being cut loose on our own and before the previous team deployed back to their home parks. The belowground workings were awesome, a true sight to behold. The access was daunting, with ladders, doors and access routes seemingly everywhere! Deep down in the dam were the inner workings, the computers, control consoles and the workers who stayed down there all shift. There were no windows or distractions. They had to control the water, hydraulics, electrical generators, sluices and so much more. It was the heart of the dam workings, and it was behind secure bulletproof and bombproof access doors. Video cameras allowed the occupants to see who was at the door before granting access.

While I was near the gift store, Dispatch radioed to me that a 911 call just came in from my assigned area. Then they gave me the report that made me realize that this was not a game, but a real-life assignment. They said they received a 911 call from the

Main Control Room, and then the phone was hung up.

I immediately responded to the elevators, calling for backup. As I passed a Dam Guide, I grabbed him and said, "You're going with me."

We headed to the elevator as I asked him if he could get me to the Main Control Room. He said he could. I explained I had only been there once before but was unsure of my way. There were no signs to helpfully direct terrorists to its location. As we entered the elevator, Dispatch called again.

"We just received a call from the Main Control Room. The reporting party (RP) states the 911 call was an accident and that everything is fine now."

"Copy," I replied. "Still responding per protocol."

Dispatch replied with "Copy," and the time.

As the elevator door closed, the guide was incredulous. Why was I still dragging him down there when he had just heard that everything was okay?

"It may well be, but it is my job to be sure. It's an old trick to put a gun to a person's head and have them call in the okay. We need to see for ourselves," I replied.

"I never thought of that," he said.

We ran from the elevator to a catwalk, then down a fight of stairs and through doors. We took another elevator and then more stairs and more doors. It was a maze and I was so very glad I had the guide with me. We moved fast but it still took us close to ten minutes to get to the Main Control Room. Once I located it, I motioned the guide back through a safe door. My radio would not get out at that location, so I approached the door with my 9mm pistol drawn and in the low-ready position. It was pointed at a 45-degree angle to the floor. That way, if I discharged it at a bad guy while raising it, I still might get them with a ricochet. Pointed at the ceiling, I didn't have that advantage.

As I approached the door, it cracked open. I ordered the man opening the door back and to show me his hands. I saw the other two in the background and they were all white as a sheet. I knew who they were as I checked their IDs on an almost daily basis. There were no strange faces. I looked quickly around as the first man explained the situation.

"We were installing new phones down here. We programmed the auto dial for 911 and it just went off. We're really sorry," he said.

"Is there anyone else here," I asked?

"No, that is really what happened," he insisted.

I asked all three to sit in their chairs and to not move. There was a walk space that surrounded the console room with access corridors. I told them I had to check them out and that they were to stay put and quiet. They all nodded their heads.

I went from corridor to side passage to rooms and hallways throughout the area. I thanked my lucky stars for the in-service, for I knew it wasn't a very large area beyond the control room and I was able to check it quickly. When I was 100% convinced there was no one there, I went back to the control room and used the phone to call Dispatch and give them our correct code for all being okay. I then sat down in a chair and sighed.

The men still apologized to me, insisting they had called Dispatch that all was okay. I relayed the gun-to-the-head possibility, and they all knew what I had meant. They were just so sorry to have put me through all of this.

"Are you kidding? This was the most excitement I've had on this damn, er, dam assignment!" I exclaimed. ❏

THE TROUT

As a Naturalist Ranger at Lodgepole in Sequoia National Park, I had the most fun telling visitors about the life that abounds in the Sierra. In particular, I gave a demonstration called *Wild World*. I had skins, bones, skulls, nests and all kinds of props. But there was nothing like the real thing. When folks saw a squirrel, Steller's jay, deer or even a bear, there was an excitement and realization that this was not a zoo. The animals could go where they wanted, when they wanted.

The camaraderie among staff was often the aspect that made work so special. Early in my career, married Rangers brought their spouses and children for the summer. Now, with housing so tight, that is rarely an option. Ranger Naturalist Vaughn brought his wife Judy and children, Chris and Amy, with him every summer. Vaughn and Judy were schoolteachers in Oregon the rest of the year. They lived in a very old, two-room government cabin and walked to a community bathroom. Their children literally grew up at Lodgepole. They were both great kids, but on the shy side. At an early age, Chris showed an interest in fly-fishing and the uncanny ability to catch just about anything he set his mind to. Chris was tall and thin, a perfect match for the bamboo pole he used to search the cool Sierra streams for trout. By the time Chris was nine, none of us knew of a better fisherman – boy, man or Ranger!

One day I asked Chris if he thought he could catch a trout for my *Wild World* demonstration. I would need it by 8:00 a.m. the next morning. He said he thought he could and I gave him a small white bucket. Sure enough, waiting outside my cabin door the next morning was the little bucket with a perky rainbow trout inside. I took it to my *Wild World* talk and released it into the Marble Fork of the Kaweah River after the demonstration. The trout was a hit. Seeing something alive was always an attraction. In addition, many of the visitors came to fish and often wanted to know the details on catching the trout. What lure, where and what techniques were used? I could give them a general idea, but Chris was too shy to come to the demonstration and talk about the trout. After that day, I had a trout in a bucket outside my cabin every morning I had a *Wild World* talk. I offered to pay Chris but he wouldn't take any money. His mom said he loved the challenge and he loved being needed. He was contributing to the program. Then, one morning of a *Wild World* talk, for the first time in several years, there was no trout. I worried about Chris, but I had to get going as the talk would start soon. I left for the Visitor Center.

* * * *

Over these same years Chris' dad, Vaughn, developed multiple sclerosis. He had become thinner and weaker, and walked with a limp. He could no longer go backpacking and regretted that he could not hike with his family anymore. The summer Chris turned 15 years old was the first summer the Sequoia Natural History Association (SNHA) offered a Trans Sierra hike to Mount Whitney. I had led many backpacking Seminars for SNHA over the years and was excited to be leading this hike. Two young boys, Tim and Ted, had gone on shorter hikes with me through SNHA. Neither parent from Solvang, California, were hikers, but they wanted their sons to have the opportunity, so they signed them up for the SNHA Trans Sierra seminar. Ted was 15, and Tim was only 12. I wasn't sure this was doable, but they really wanted to go. Ted promised Tim would make it even if he had to carry him. Then I had an idea.

I went to the Chief Naturalist, John, who also was coordinating SNHA. I told John that this was the first Trans Sierra Seminar and there were some issues still to be worked out, but that I needed him to pay $150 for an assistant. When I told him my plan, he readily agreed. I then sought out Vaughn, Judy and Chris. I explained that I was leading this 9-day seminar and that it was full. It was mostly adults, but also two young boys. I needed Chris to go with me to teach fly-fishing, be a companion to the boys, carry supplies and be the caboose on the trip so I would have no stragglers. They all thought it was a great idea, and then I added that Chris would be paid. It was a small fortune to him. The trip was a fabulous success. My brother Dan joined us and the whole group formed a friendship that lasted a long time. One gal even celebrated her fortieth birthday on top of Mount Whitney! I brought a candle and she had a muffin. We all sang Happy Birthday with the candle struggling in the thin air. Chris was irreplaceable. He made his mark at Wallace Creek. Here, the elusive golden trout were rumored to reside. Chris set up his tackle and took those interested in fishing to the stream. I watched as Chris, not used to being the center of attention, mumbled a bit about technique, and then let his pole do the talking. On his first cast, it was a mere second before he had a gorgeous golden trout dancing on the end of his line. Everyone laughed and applauded. Then patiently, Chris went from person to person and coached them. They all eventually caught trout and had a grand supper with fish stories being told long into the night.

* * * *

But this morning, three years before the SNHA trip, the morning of my *Wild World* talk, there was no trout in a bucket at my cabin door. I assembled my demonstration and welcomed my group of fifty visitors who were sitting on benches in front of the Visitor Center. As I started, the group turned their heads in the direction of the river and watched as a tall, lean boy came running toward me with a bamboo fishing pole and a small white bucket, splashing water out of the sides. It was Chris, who arrived just in time with a most beautiful rainbow trout. It was too big for the bucket, its tail above one rim and his head above the other as the fish arched from side to side. Chris put the bucket down and folks clamored to see the trout. The folks, especially men, began to ask Chris questions about bait, line, pole and technique. Chris answered their questions and stood a bit taller as he did so. He was in his element, talking about fishing. I finally got the visitors back into their seats and talked a bit about the biology of trout. Then I thanked Chris and asked him if he would release the trout into the river. As he walked away with his bucket and pole, the crowd enthusiastically applauded.

I later found Chris to ask what had happened. He was so apologetic. He had overslept, he explained. When he realized he was late, he threw on a T-shirt, grabbed his pole and bucket, and ran down the hill to the river. In one motion, he filled the bucket with water and made a cast, instantly catching a rainbow trout. He usually tried to fish until he caught me a small one that fit the bucket, but he didn't think he had time today. So with this 12-inch goliath, dripping out of the bucket, he ran up the slope to my *Wild World*. He was only 13 years of age at the time, but remains to this day, the finest fisherman I have ever known. ❑

Extrication

One of the good things about living at the Grand Canyon is the generally mild winters. When I lived in the Sierra Nevada Mountains, the snow persisted and you could snowshoe and cross country ski for weeks. On the South Rim, I learned I had to ski while it was snowing or within the first few days because it melted so quickly. My first season was the exception, when Kent and I put sawhorses up to close East Rim Drive, the road to Desert View. This was prior to the gate that now serves that purpose. I distinctly remember the snow coming to mid-thigh on me in some places, and that was unusual. I never saw it that deep again in over fifteen years of winters on the canyon rim.

But what did occur in the winter, and all too frequently, was black ice and frozen snow on the roads. It was beyond slick at times and highly dangerous. I came on shift as the Acting Shift Supervisor on January 9, at 5:00 p.m. Even before I could make it to briefing, Dispatch toned out a report of a motor vehicle accident (MVA), south of the town of Tusayan. This was prior to the establishment of the Tusayan Fire Department and the presence of Guardian Ambulance in the town. For decades, the National Park Service responded outside the park to assist our neighbors in mutual aid. I had just pulled up to Station One when John, from the dayshift, said he would drive the ambulance. I grabbed my firefighter turnouts and told him I would respond in my patrol car and give an initial size-up. From Dispatch's second call it sounded bad, with at least two cars involved and people trapped in a vehicle. The sun was setting, the snow and the air temperature were falling and the roads were icing up. I asked for a General Alarm to get more folks to bring the other ambulance, extrication vehicle and fire engine. I took Incident Command (IC) as I headed out of the park. Once I was in the town of Tusayan, the roads were nearly undriveable. As careful as I was, I felt like I was on an air hockey table, just gliding by. I received a call from Peggy, a firefighter who had her turnouts with her in Tusayan, and slowed to pick her up in front of the old Moqui Lodge. I was only going five miles per hour and still slid past her to a stop. She threw herself into the front seat and put on her seatbelt as we crawled down the highway. It was agonizingly slow, and I called in to all responding units to take great care. The really scary thing was there was no oncoming traffic. That usually meant an accident was so bad that people could not drive around it to continue on their way.

I soon received a report from Department of Public Safety (DPS) Officer Gary that he was en route and the same from Coconino County Sheriff's Deputy (CCSO) Jim that he was almost on scene. Tusayan Airport Fire Crew also gathered to respond and, all tolled, we had an army of almost 25 responding personnel. We just had to get there. The snow was coming down sideways and the road was pure ice. About twelve miles south, I came across a horrendous scene. DPS and CCSO had moved non-involved cars to a single lane and backed them up so responding emergency vehicles could get to the wreckage. There was a large, full-sized truck with an open bed stopped in the middle of the road and, in front of it, a Jeep Cherokee. It had been hit in the side and had crumpled badly. The side impact had turned its cross-section from a square to a diamond. It was later measured, and the distance in the back seat from the right side to the left side was only 19 inches. I talked to Gary and Jim and received a scene size-up. I walked around the Jeep and could see one seat in front of the other, lined up like dominoes. I learned that one young child, about 6 years old, was now in a bystander's sedan. I asked Peggy to assess the patient and let me know what she needed. It was now dark and I approached the crumpled Jeep with my flashlight.

There was no real visible front seat. The passenger's headrest was against the dash.

I could hear the voice of a woman from under the passenger dash and she was calling out, "My babies! Help my babies."

I quickly reassured her we would and said I would be right back. On the driver's side, I could see a male's head trapped between the headrest and the steering wheel and it was not looking good. I reached in and could feel a pulse, but could not reach much else of him. He didn't respond when I called out to him. I then went to the right side of the vehicle on the back passenger side. I could reach in and feel the far door with little effort. I had my turnouts on and felt the glass tumble under my arm as I reached across. It appeared the seat right behind the front was unoccupied, but it had crushed back onto a little girl.

She was sitting smack in the middle of the back seat, pinned by the seat in front of her and the crushed sides of the vehicle. Because the roof had lifted in the middle to make the top of the diamond, I could crawl in a bit to see her. Her eyes were open and they matched the color of her curly brown hair. Only her head was visible and as I started to talk to her, her eyes never moved. Her pupils were dilated and then I saw the gaping hole above her eyes. The skin had separated into a long side-to-side gash revealing frontal bone. Between the broken bones was visible brain matter exuding from her skull. I shook my head as I had mistaken this for hair bangs in the darkened vehicle. I felt and found a weak carotid pulse in her neck, but I knew she was gone.

John arrived with the ambulance and a crew and I sent him to the dad. I called out an update to Dispatch about the number of victims and that my priority was extrication. The responding units all acknowledged, but they were driving agonizingly slow to the scene. John came over to me and said he needed help with patient care. I turned to Chris and asked if he would take over IC so I could work as a paramedic and he said yes. We transferred by radio so all knew to call Chris from now on and I went to the dad. John had trouble maintaining an airway because blood was coming from the dad's nose and mouth. He was gurgling and it was fairly apparent that, in addition to a head injury, he had a crush injury to his chest. I went to the ambulance and got an endotracheal tube. With the dad in an upright position, I gently inserted the tube through a nostril and along his palate. I was worried about a possible basal skull fracture, but I felt this was my only option. I put the end of the tube next to my cheek so I could feel the patient's exhalations as I lowered it past his vocal cords and into his trachea. When I was sure I was in, I inflated the bulb with a 10cc syringe and we auscultated (listened with a stethoscope) for lung sounds. We heard them loud and clear and watched the chest move as we supplied him oxygen with a bag-valve mask.

I then went around to the mom and asked how she was. She was only moaning now, not saying any deliberate words, but she was still alive. I then went into the car and reached over to the little girl in the back. Her pulse was absent, and she was gone. Peggy found me and I went to the sedan to listen to her assessment of the minor injuries to the little boy. He would be okay and Peggy was doing a great job with his care. I then learned from Gary that the driver of the truck that hit the Jeep was upset. I asked Gary what happened to cause this scene. From his preliminary investigation, witnesses stated the Jeep was traveling north toward the canyon at a high rate of speed, passing people. It finally slid out of control on the snow and ice and slid sideways into the southbound truck. Gary didn't feel the truck driver was at fault. The Jeep was traveling too fast for the conditions.

I went to the driver of the truck and asked if he was okay. He had been assessed by two EMTs at this point and was physically uninjured. He was in tears when he learned there were children in the car. He probably knew he wasn't at fault but, still, he was involved and it would haunt him forever.

By the time I returned to the Jeep, the Fire Crew had arrived and my Kent had them taking their positions to take off the roof. They covered all the passengers, took out what was left of the windshield, and cut all of the supporting posts after chocking the vehicle. Within six minutes, they were carrying the roof of the Jeep off to the side of the road. Chuck then leaned in and, in pulling the tarp off the back seat, saw the little girl. I assured him she was gone, but I could see it really affected him. There were several parents on the brigade with children in this age group and it was devastating, especially with what we had to do next.

While one crew worked on the passenger's front door to get to the mom, I worked with another to release the dad. The extrication crew used a pulley system to yank the steering wheel off his chest, but the side door was crumpled into him. We could easily pull him up and out now that the roof was gone, and that is what we planned. But the little girl was in the way and her body was still trapped inside. I put several blankets over her, but we all knew she was there. We couldn't waste time taking her little body out to delay extricating a living passenger. We slipped the backboard under the dad and tilted it down onto the blankets over his daughter as we pulled him onto the board. Chuck tried so hard to hold the board so it wouldn't crush her to get him out. We pulled the dad out and took him to the ambulance to head back to the canyon. We were closer to the Grand Canyon Clinic, which was then manned 24-hours by physicians and nurses. There he could be stabilized and then sent south to Flagstaff Medical Center. Besides, the roads were not safe to the south. It was jammed for miles with ice and snow and traffic. The little boy was already on his way when I received word that they had popped the door on the front passenger side to release the mom. When they gently pulled her out and put her on a backboard, she died within seconds. The ALS crew with her started IVs and did CPR, but it was no use. Her crumpled position under the dash had put pressure on the torn internal organs and arteries. Once she was "unfolded," that pressure was gone and she bled to death in seconds.

We got our patient to the Clinic where he was stabilized and eventually transferred to Flagstaff Medical Center. He died the next day of an inoperable brain bleed. The lone little boy was left without an entire family because someone just had to get somewhere, now. Grown men and women cried on each other's shoulders that night. Innocent lives lost – for what?

CANOE

The Everglades has incredible resources. Prior to Hurricane Andrew, Eco Pond at Flamingo had so many bird species, it was near impossible to give a nature hike without being interrupted by two or three rare or unique species while trying to interpret a third. Smooth-billed Anis would vie with Roseate Spoonbills, Lazuli Buntings and Harrier Hawks, not to mention other animals such as alligators and rattlesnakes. One of my most fun, interpretive activities was taking folks in canoes on the Bear Lake Canal. It was a surreal adventure through mangrove swamps mixed with hundreds of other plants, birds and land species. You never knew what was going to be around the next corner. Set back from the water's edge on higher ground were the Gumbo Limbo trees. They were nicknamed the "tourist trees" as their red bark would peel, not unlike a tourist who had been in the sun too long.

I had had some experience canoeing and hauling a trailer, but we Rangers all received a course on the basics of handling a canoe and how to drive and back a trailer. We used a trailer to haul the six to eight canoes to the parking spot at the canal input, and had to back it in so it was a straight shot out. Because of the limited space, signups for the activity were required and there was always a waiting list. We met folks at the Flamingo Visitor Center and then carpooled to the input area. Once there, I gave a safety briefing, handed out life vests and gave a basic in-service on handling canoes.

On one particular drizzly morning, we had a full group of several families. The dividing of the families was usually pretty easy, as it was today. One set of parents had two little girls, aged eight and seven, and no one had canoe experience. So I had the parents go together and I took the two girls in my canoe, as I could paddle it by myself. The others in the group sorted out nicely. We put the canoes in, and I took the lead as the other six behind me followed the parents' canoe. Despite the on-and-off drizzle, the canopy of vegetation gave an otherworldly feel to the trek. We saw birds galore and mangrove crabs and oysters on prop roots. In areas where the canal widened into small pond-like areas, I was able to gather the group and give information on what they may have seen or what to anticipate ahead. About thirty minutes into the trip it began to rain rather than drizzle, and I asked if everyone was game to go on, as I sure was. They all answered with an enthusiastic "Yes!" which made us all laugh. We knew not many got to canoe in the Everglades and we were all prepared for the inclement weather with slickers and hats.

As we set off, I heard thunder roar in the distance. We were entering a narrower area of the canal that allowed only one canoe to pass at a time, and I had stressed the importance of leaving some distance between canoes. So, as we snaked our way through the maze, no canoe could see the one in front or behind. It was a truly eerie and adventurous feeling. As I paddled the youngsters upstream, the calm, warm rain was interrupted by an instantaneous blinding flash of light and a crush of thunder that exploded over us. Plant material, leaves and branches tumbled into our canoe as the two girls screamed in terror. Then I heard screaming behind me as their parents called their girls' names in fright. I had stopped the canoe and ducked down over the girls as a reflex when the lightning had struck. I now waited for the parents to come to within sight of us to see that we were okay.

The girls threatened to upset us as they wanted the comfort of their folk's laps, but we talked them down and I began a feigned laugh at what an incredible experience it was.

As I looked around in the rain, I saw a smoldering Gumbo Limbo tree to my left not thirteen feet away. It had been blown to smithereens, throwing bits of it and other vegetation into our canoe. We all paddled into the next open pond area, and I took branches and leaves and twigs out of the bottom of the canoe while I waited for the others to catch up. With a sigh of relief, I told them we would be heading back because of the lightning threat. All agreed it was the right thing to do, and we returned in under an hour. We spent time at the put-in area talking about lightning and Mother Nature and things we would never be able to control. By this time, everyone was cheerful and laughing again with a heck of a story to tell. ❏

Bounty Hunters

We had a fairly large community on the South Rim of the Grand Canyon. There were several thousand residents and a school that hosted kindergarten through twelfth grade. The South Rim Rangers started a co-ed Explorer Troop. We had the opportunity to work with high school students in many venues. We taught them First Aid and CPR, how to assist on Search and Rescue (SAR) scenes, and even how to climb. One student, Jacob, I had known almost all of his life. As a teenager he turned out to be a fabulous young man. His sister Erin helped me as a language interpreter on several calls. One gorgeous summer day, Jacob and I were on the cliffs by the Bright Angel Lodge off of West Rim Drive. Jacob had progressed so quickly in SAR skills that we decided he was up to a free rappel – a rappel without a cliff face, just rope and air. We secured our anchors, belay and rappel lines, and I settled in to belay Jacob. Off he went, over the edge, and he worked his way down. He had admitted to me he was a bit nervous, but he was a pro when it came to the actual event. While he was changing over to ascend back up the rope, I glanced at the sky above me and there were two condors right above us.

"Hey, Jacob, can you see the condors?" I called.

He quickly replied, "What are you doing looking at condors when I am down here?"

I chuckled at his nervous response. He soon outpaced me as a free climber and later went to college to become a Ranger himself.

Another Explorer was Samuel. Samuel was a smart young man, and he loved to go on ride-a-longs with the Rangers. One clear summer day, Samuel joined me in my patrol car. We talked about observing, looking for things out of the ordinary. We talked about the law and how I couldn't just pull anyone over I wanted to. I explained we had to have a reasonable suspicion that a crime was being or had been committed. Often, small infractions are used to get to bigger issues.

We had left my residence where I had made us bologna sandwiches and were driving through the residential area. In front of us, headed in our direction, was a bright yellow Cadillac with Louisiana plates. There were three very large men in the vehicle, two in the front and one in the back right seat. As they passed us, I asked Samuel to tell me what was wrong with "this picture." Samuel quickly replied that it wasn't a resident's car. All of the teenage boys seem to know everybody on the South Rim by their vehicle. I watched in my rearview mirror as the Cadillac made an illegal U-turn. I pulled over as they passed me and turned on my rotating patrol lights to pull them over, calling the license plate into Park Dispatch. The vehicle pulled over, and I pulled in behind it as I waited for a return from Dispatch that said there were no wants or warrants for the vehicle. Samuel knew to stay in the car but watched as I exited and approached on the driver's side, stopping at the back left passenger window. I didn't want to be in front of the rear passenger where I could not see his hands or movements. I greeted the driver and he was forced to turn around in his seat to speak with me. He was huge, easily over 400 pounds. The other two men were no lightweights either. With a Southern accent, the driver greeted me and thrust a clipboard in my direction. On it was a "Wanted" poster for a 45-year-old female.

"Have you seen this woman, Officer?" the driver asked.

Ignoring his question, I asked him for his driver's license and registration along with proof of insurance. I also asked the other two occupants to place their hands in plain sight where I could see them. They immediately complied. The driver fumbled for a while and finally came up with the requested documents. I called the information in to Dispatch and spoke to the driver.

"Why are you looking for this woman?" I asked.

"She is wanted and we're bounty hunters. We got a tip she was in the park and we're gonna find her, then call America's Most Wanted and then they're gonna film us takin' her down," he said proudly.

I asked him for his permit to conduct business in a National Park and he said he didn't need one, that he was a bounty hunter and could go anywhere. I explained that wasn't true in this case. I asked if he had secured a film permit to have the film crew in the park. He looked perplexed at this.

I quickly asked him the question I was waiting to slip in and said, "Well, if you're a bounty hunter, where is your gun?"

He immediately froze and I could see he was weighing his answer.

"I don't have a gun, Officer," he finally replied.

"Well," I said, "I only let folks lie to me once. If you lie again, then you are interfering with my ability to conduct a lawful investigation and you could be arrested for interference ... where is your gun? You have only one more chance to answer me truthfully."

He let out a breath and said it was in a case in the trunk. I asked him for the car keys and asked the passengers if they had any weapons, and they both denied it. The driver disagreed as he handed me the keys, and told me the gun in the trunk belonged to the rear passenger.

I cautioned them not to move and to keep their hands where I could see them. I took the car keys and retreated to my patrol car, explaining briefly my findings to Dispatch and asking for backup. Samuel was riveted on the suspect vehicle, my second set of eyes. When backup arrived, they put Samuel in the rear patrol vehicle, farthest from the suspects, and then took up cover positions. I approached the car, opened the trunk, and took out a black case with a loaded Glock pistol inside. I unloaded the pistol and put it in my trunk. Dispatch then came back over the radio with a warrant for the driver. It was not clear to Dispatch whether it was a felony or misdemeanor warrant, but it was for writing bad checks worth over $5,000, no bail, and that Louisiana would extricate. The passengers came back clear. More backup came and Samuel was taken away from the dangerous situation, much to his chagrin. I carefully approached the driver.

"Well, John," I said, "Louisiana wants you."

I explained the warrant, the illegality of having a loaded

weapon in a National Park and illegal bounty hunting in the park without a permit.

I then said, "We can do this the easy way, or we can do this the hard way. You can see all of my backup. If you do everything I say when I say it, no one will get hurt. If you do not cooperate, you may end up on the pavement." He got the message.

"I want to do this the easy way, Ma'am," he answered.

I cautioned the passengers to sit still and backed toward my vehicle. I then gave John the orders to exit the vehicle and back up toward mine. He truly extricated himself from the vehicle, unfolding his huge bulk from the driver's interior, and the car rose a good three inches when he exited. He was tall and big. Then he backed up, following my commands, and reached a safe area behind the suspect vehicle. My colleagues took him into custody, searching him and handcuffing him. It took two sets of cuffs linked together to secure his hands behind his back.

Once he was headed to booking, I returned to the Cadillac. The other two were meek and cooperative. The back passenger wanted to set the record straight, that it was not his gun. John said it was because John had a prior felony conviction and was a prohibited possessor, (not allowed to have a firearm in his possession), another violation for John. I told the passengers they were free to leave. I suggested they look at the canyon and then leave the park without looking for the wanted person so they would not have any more contact with Rangers. They both agreed and said they were leaving immediately. The last I saw the Cadillac it was heading south, out of the park.

OC

Fred and I worked extremely well together. He was an excellent EMT and, in law enforcement situations, we often knew what move the other would take so we could anticipate each other's needs. We had arrived to a dispute call at one of the dorms for the concession employees. We split up and went upstairs in Rouzer Hall. We saw several people speaking loudly, not quite yelling, outside a room that had its door open.

I identified myself and asked what was going on. The talkers were so engrossed they did not see my approach. As soon as a 30-year-old man with a fanny pack saw me, he started to walk away down the hall. But Fred was waiting for him and asked him to stop. The two women the man had been talking to retreated to their room, but stuck their heads out to watch the proceedings. I asked the man if he lived at Rouzer Hall and he said no. I asked him where he lived and he didn't answer. I asked him if he worked at the Grand Canyon and he said no. I told him that it was late at night and he needed a Guest Permit to visit or stay in the dorm after hours. The Fire and Safety personnel were down the hallway and nodded their head in agreement. I then asked the man for identification, and he said he would just rather leave. I told him he was trespassing and that I needed to know who I was talking to and that this could easily be resolved if he cooperated.

He carefully reached down to his fanny pack and slowly unzipped the outer pouch. Suddenly, a slew of small baggies with a white powdery substance fell to the ground. He looked up startled, then ran toward Fred, stopped and ran back toward me. He was obviously a drug dealer.

Fred had his pepper spray, oleoresin capsaicin (OC), hidden in his hand and I knew this.

"Spray him, Fred!" I called.

Fred ran and sprayed the suspect just as he was approaching me. A cloud of OC flew into the air hitting the suspect and then me. Fred's momentum carried him into the cloud. The suspect ran into the women's dorm room, pushed the screen out of an open window, and straddled the windowsill with one leg in and the other out. I began to hack and cough, but my contact lenses or perhaps closing my eyes in time preserved my vision. I tried to speak but little came out. I motioned to the Fire and Safety personnel to go downstairs below the window. I called to the suspect who was coughing and hacking. I looked at Fred. His eyes were tightly shut and I put my hand on his shoulder. He could talk but not see; I could see but not talk.

I forced my voice out at a squeak and asked Fred if he was okay. He nodded his head and was trying very hard to open his eyes. I turned my attention to the suspects, ordering mostly with gestures and a dry, hacking voice for the two women to lie on the floor. They quickly complied.

"Get off the window sill and lie down on the ground," I barked out in broken syllables to the suspect.

His voice was clearer than mine and he responded, "Come any closer and I'll jump."

"Go ahead, jump," I said, "and we'll pick your sorry ass up at the bottom and take you to the hospital before we take you to jail."

I have no idea where my response came from, (normally I'm not so gruff), but it was genuine at the time. The suspect seemed to believe me and slowly came back into the room. I grabbed him and pushed him to the ground. Fred had his eyes open halfway, tearing like mad, and so I held the suspect in an arm lock while Fred handcuffed him behind his back.

I called Park Dispatch and, in a ragged voice, said we had one in custody, that we were not Code Four (that is radio lingo for "we're okay") and needed immediate backup. We blinked and coughed and held our own until backup arrived. Yep, Fred and I were a good team. ❏

Personal Injury

I once heard a disabled person call the rest of the world TABs: Temporarily Able-Bodied. We all have times in our lives when we are incapacitated and not able to function as we would like. It could be a flu bug or twisted ankle, or something more severe. When you are a Park Ranger, there are plenty of hazardous situations that can contribute to personal injury. In law enforcement, we said there were four lights: green, yellow, orange and red. Green is off-duty, safely in your home without a care in the world. You should never, ever be green on duty. The very least you should be is yellow. Yellow is cautious, aware, observant and not easily distracted. Orange is when there is the potential for a threat situation. You are on your guard. You maintain your space from people, especially suspects. You are in your FI or Field Interrogation stance. Your body is bladed, your knees loose with good balance; your gun, in its holster, is oriented away from suspects, and your arm is adjacent to it without being obvious. You are in LE (Law Enforcement) mode and focused on the threat and the situation around you. You are aware of your tactics, the levels of force available to you and how you will react to protect yourself and others. You also know where your escape corridor runs. Red is all action, all events happening right now, in a blaze and often with yelling, screaming, fighting and, at times, weapons. You hope you always make the right decisions in red, as it all happens so very fast. This is where your training pays off, and your reactions and muscle memory kick in.

You hope never to get to red. I relied a lot on a concept called "verbal judo." It's the art of talking to folks so they know you mean business; you are mentally stronger and therefore physically stronger, no matter the size of the suspect. You try to keep events from going to red, but if they do, you try to minimize injury to yourself, the suspect and bystanders. If a suspect bolts while you are questioning and about to arrest him or her, the natural instinct is to give chase. In one instance, I ran after a suspect and when I was nearly on top of him, I didn't tackle him. That would have brought us both crashing to the ground into the rocks. Instead, I pushed him while he was running. That was enough to place him off balance and tumble alone to the ground where I could subdue and cuff him. In another running instance, it was quickly apparent the suspect was faster than I, so I stopped. I got on the radio and called in his description and direction of travel and, within minutes, colleagues were waiting for him. But neither of these techniques works when the suspect does not run away from but toward you.

Outside of the Maswik Lodge at the canyon, an intoxicated male about 40 years of age was panhandling for money from the tourists. On my arrival, he was observed to be loud, offensive in speech, and swaying and stumbling. I got within a few feet of him when two more Rangers, Kristen and Dave, arrived. I asked the suspect if we could talk to him "over here," pointing away from the crowd of people. He turned to me and said, "F— you!" and then walked with purpose toward me. By law, a commissioned officer cannot be offended by the use of expletives toward them. But this suspect had uttered it loud enough so the whole crowd could hear him. He did us a favor by committing this misdemeanor in our presence – disorderly conduct. Now we had the right to detain and even arrest him. I again ordered him to the area away from the crowd, and he continued toward me. Kristen stepped in from behind him and put him in a perfect arm lock before he could reach me. I took his other arm and he began to jump and kick and spit at us. We took him to the ground and he was still kicking, with steel-toed cowboy boots. This could cause a big-time injury to officers. Dave sat on the suspect's legs and pulled off his boots as we struggled to get him into position to handcuff him. The entire time this was going on, Kristen and I repeated the words we were taught in control tactics.

"Calm down, sir. We don't want you to hurt yourself or others ... calm down, sir."

It was like a mantra. We never yelled at him, never called him a bad name, never hit him, just controlled him and kept saying our mantra. It never got through to him, but after he was cuffed and we sat up to catch our breath, we looked around to see no fewer than ten video cameras on us from the crowd. The mantra protected us, gave us something to say other than what we really wanted to say and, perhaps, got through to a suspect. Luckily, no one was hurt that day.

One of my earliest mishaps at the Grand Canyon did not involve a LE incident. One morning we received a call of a plane that was on a sightseeing tour that had to make a forced landing in the woods. I suppose you could say it crashed, but it was a controlled crash. I had been called out of a deep sleep at home, threw on my flight suit and boots and responded to the helibase. Several of us flew outside the park on a mutual aid response and found the six-seater in a field of sagebrush. No one was killed, although most were walking wounded. I was assigned a 52-year-old male who had a back injury, but had the use of his arms and legs. We packaged him with full spinal precautions and flew by helicopter to the South Rim Helibase. The staff at the Grand Canyon Clinic was waiting for us. Once we got into the ambulance for the three-minute ride to the clinic, I suddenly felt a searing, stabbing pain on top of my left thigh just above the knee. It felt like a hot poker piercing my skin. I grabbed my thigh and winced as a second hot stab hit me. This time I cried out.

"Are you okay?" my patient asked.

"Yes, just a cramp, I think," I replied as the hot jab hit me again and again. Tears came to my eyes but I kept my composure, hitting at my thigh over and over again. When we arrived at the clinic, one of the nurses opened the door as I launched myself out of the back of the ambulance and through the clinic doors. I unzipped my flight suit and pulled it to my ankles. I watched as bits and pieces of a scorpion tumbled to the floor at my feet. The doctor came out and said, "Whoa!"

A large red welt started to form, but the searing hot pain was gone. I pulled my fight suit up and gave report as the others wheeled my patient into a treatment room. The doctor returned to me after she had seen the patient and wanted to see my thigh again. It was angry, red and swollen, but I showed no sign of hives or breathing difficulties. There was no hint of an allergic reaction. Still, to be on the safe side, she wanted to give me an antihistamine. My supervisor showed up to do the Workman's Compensation paperwork (an on-the-job injury), as they started a quick IV and gave me 50mg of Benadryl (an antihistamine). I was never one for taking medications, and 25mg of Benadryl by mouth has been known to put me to sleep. They called my husband Kent, who had also returned from the crash site, to take me home. The Benadryl did the trick. I never had an allergic reaction, but I didn't wake up to a state of coherency until the following evening! I can only surmise the scorpion was in my flight suit or boot when I put it on. I usually shake my clothes and shoes to prevent an unwanted hitchhiker, but I was in too much of a hurry to check that morning.

Sometimes there are minor little injuries, like getting your finger caught in a door, or fiberglass in your hands. The railroad gates on West Rim Drive were stuck in the down position one afternoon. I went over and lifted them up and out of the way. It wasn't until I lowered the gates again, that I realized I should have worn gloves. I had hundreds of tiny fiberglass slivers in my palms and fingers. The remedy is the same as small cactus spines. I poured white glue on my hands and waited until it hardened. When I peeled it off, it took most of the slivers with it.

One sunny morning we received a report of a large motorhome on fire at the South Entrance Station. We responded to the Fire Station, turned out in our bunkers (fire-fighting protective clothes), and hopped into the engine for the ride. On our arrival there was smoke coming from the front engine compartment. Tammy and I put on our self-contained breathing apparatus (SCBA) and made our approach. With a charged hose line, we lifted the hood just a bit, but smoke continued at a leisurely pace. We disconnected the battery cables and took the heavy hose full of water to the side door. As we looked inside, there was a gray haze. We went to the console between the driver and passenger front seats and removed the hood. Something just below was on fire, but we couldn't see the source. We didn't want to cause excess water damage, so I volunteered to get the carbon dioxide extinguisher off the engine.

I was back in a flash and Tammy was back by the door with the charged line as I made my approach. I aimed the extinguisher at the engine compartment we had opened. I sprayed it once and the smoke banked down. I then removed the cover to the air filter. I aimed the extinguisher and depressed the nozzle again. As the gas burst from the extinguisher, there was an immediate large blue arc of electricity that threw me back against the bulkhead of the motorhome. Tammy estimated the distance at six feet. I slid down the wall and dropped the extinguisher, stunned by what had happened. Tammy helped me up and out of the vehicle. She called to our LE Specialist Dave, who had been in the area, that I might have been electrocuted. As I walked toward the engine, my legs felt rubbery and tingly. He asked if I was all right as I slumped to my knees. It was as if I had no control over them.

"I guess not," I replied.

Dave helped me to the back of the ambulance. I felt a little better and sat in the back for a bit. It was decided they would transport me to the clinic as a precaution. On the way there, I put myself on the heart monitor; the Ranger with me was not trained in ACLS. My back was a bit sore from hitting the wall with my SCBA tank, but I was cleared at the clinic and was able to immediately return to work. As it turned out, the owner of the motorhome had three, 12-volt batteries tied in series to power appliances in his vehicle. When we disconnected the motor battery, it didn't affect the appliance batteries and I received quite a jolt. I learned a valuable lesson. My colleagues gave me a teddy bear named Arc, Jr., and called me Sparky for the longest time.

Over a decade of work at the Grand Canyon has given me my share of bumps and bruises. But the next I inflicted on myself. My husband Kent and I had just acquired our Golden Retriever puppy, Shannon. It was October and I was on the night shift. When I woke about 10:00 a.m., I often did chores. It was time to build her a fence. I had gotten clearance from the housing office and we had purchased the posts, fencing, and gate. I had a ten-pound sledgehammer I was using to put the stakes into the hard Kaibab limestone. It was about 3:00 p.m. when I began to tire. On the last stake of the day, I held the handle next to the head and brought it down with as much force as I could muster. On the second stroke, my right thumb somehow ended up between the ten-pound hammer and the metal stake. When I hit my thumb, the hammer went flying and an involuntary epithet came to my lips. I don't often swear, but I did this time. I like to say to people that I only said one bad word . . . but I said it over and over and over again.

Then the pain went away and blood trickled out of my leather work glove. I gingerly pulled it off to reveal a smashed thumbnail and broken skin. It became numb and didn't hurt anymore. So I cleaned it up and got ready for work. Everyday when I put my duty belt on, I would take the magazine out of my 9mm pistol and pull the slide back to eject the chambered round. I would double-check it for emptiness, and then mock discharge the empty weapon by pulling the trigger with the gun aimed at the floor. It was my daily test to ensure it was all functioning well. I would then put the magazine back, cycle a round into the chamber, release the magazine and top it off with a round. Then I would release the hammer, place it back into my holster and secure it with its snap strap. But on this particular day I couldn't even release the snap strap with my right thumb to start the daily test. My thumb had no strength and it hurt like the dickens when I put pressure on it. I called Dispatch to say I would be delayed coming into service and walked the ten minutes to the clinic. There, after x-rays, the doctor confirmed I had broken my thumb in three places, placed it in a thumb splint and put me on antibiotics. I was out of service a bit longer than just that shift.

* * * *

The days I was assigned horse patrol were some of my happiest. After morning briefing with my other Ranger colleagues, I returned to the stables to begin the preparation. Just the ritual of spending about forty-five minutes preparing the horse and tack were wonderful. I took off my defensive equipment and stepped into coveralls. I then went into the corral to select my mount. Today it was Sage. Sage was older and bigger than the other mounts. But he was still fast and could tolerate most things that might make other horses skittish. I could sit by the train when it released its brakes with a long hiss and he would stand like a statue. Over the past few months though, he had been a bit off. In attempting to cross the railroad tracks by the Maswik Lodge one day, he refused to cross the tracks set into the asphalt. They weren't even raised tracks, but he would not go forward. When I insisted, he began to walk backward. Here is when we had what I like to call "a discussion." With horses it's imperative that the rider win every discussion. Once they realize they might get their way, there would be more discussions. If a patrol horse were ever to realize he is 1,400 pounds bigger than I am, that would be the end of their usefulness as a patrol horse. My technique was quick and effective.

I had been riding horses since I was three years old. I remember riding bareback on Sam as a youngster. We were told not to ride double so, in my older brother's logic, that did not prevent three on Sam. So we were tripled up and within seconds were bucked off. I learned to 'read' horses after that ... and to ignore my older brother when he came up with interesting suggestions. As a teenager I worked at a local stable. My first job was mucking them out and replacing the soiled hay. I was in heaven. Then I painted stalls and graduated to exercising clients' horses that were boarded there. There was one Shetland pony named Hombre. He was little but feisty, and too small for a saddle. That was where all my experience riding bareback paid off. In a corral that was four-sided, equaling a square, I rode Hombre for his exercise. I only had a pad on him and he just loved to run. But he didn't run in circles like other horses. Whenever he came to a corner of the corral he made a quick right turn that whipped me to the side with incredible G-forces. Every corner was a whiplash. Even anticipating the turn wasn't helpful. But I persevered. Sure I was thrown, but I got back up and fell less and less. I was then given other horses to work out and finally, two years later, I became a horse guide. Folks would come for a horse ride and I would match them to a mount and take them out on a three-hour tour. Life didn't get any better than that for a teen who loved horses.

So when Sage decided to shy away from the tracks, I reined him to the side into a full circle, then to the other side into another full circle, and then repeated both. Finally I released him, gave him his head, and gently heeled him in the side to go forward and we crossed the tracks. I don't know if I made him dizzy, distracted him so he didn't realize he was crossing the tracks, or if he learned he would never, ever win a discussion with me.

I started my ritual by cleaning his hooves after securing him to a rubber tire tied to the corral fence. That way he could have his head, if he jerked, there was some give without hurting himself or breaking the rope. I used a pick to clean each hoof in succession, always in the same order. Most horses like routine in their preparation rituals. This gelding (a neutered male horse) was no exception. Then I currycombed his coat and brushed his mane and tail. We usually only gave them baths before parades when they really needed to shine. I sprayed on purple (a topical medication) on any healing cuts, and then rubbed his eyes with my thumbs. He loved this. It removed the crusty sleepers and tears and gave a good scratch to an itchy area. I then sprayed him with a potion to keep flies off his coat and face. The pad was next. I always turned it over to make sure there were no pine needles or stickers on it that would poke into his back. Then, the saddle was placed and cinched. Sage was so tall, over sixteen hands, that I had to get a swinging momentum going to get the saddle on his back. I then cleaned the saddle and bridle and reins with saddle soap to shine. After all of this, I went to the tack room, took off my coveralls, replaced my defensive equipment, shined my boots and put on my epaulet whistle. The whistle was on a braided cord that threaded through my shoulder epaulet and then placed in my pocket. The Horse Patrol Coordinator, Ronnie, gave it to me after I completed his Horse Patrol in-service and was okayed to go forth alone in the program. I was so proud of that little whistle. Looking sharp as Horse Patrol was as much a public relations function as anything else. I put Sage's bridle on and walked him out of the preparation corral. We walked a bit first. Like many saddled horses, Sage would inhale to expand his ribs when the saddle was first cinched. If not retightened, the saddle could slide once he released his breath. Now I cinched the saddle down, mounted up and called Horse Patrol in-service to Dispatch.

The day was overcast early. The monsoon summer rains were a welcome relief to the heat, but the torrential rain could be so severe that for several minutes at a time you couldn't see your hand in front of your face. I had my slicker tied to the saddle, along with saddlebags that contained first aid items, a ticket book, water and lunch. I worked my way to the Rim Walk along the Grand Canyon and greeted visitors and answered questions. I arrived at Yavapai Museum and entered the re-vegetation area outside the front entrance. With the halter rope I kept in the saddlebag, I tied Sage to the top of the ten-foot-long section of fencing that was held at each end by a post buried deeply into the soil. It wasn't raining yet, but it looked ominous. I could hear thunder in the distance. I climbed through the fence and greeted Ranger Interpreters Mike and Marianne. Folks came up to ask us questions and we chatted for a while. As the storm got closer, I decided I better start back to the corral so Sage and I wouldn't get too soaked. I climbed back through the fence just as a nearby lightning strike flashed. I quickly stepped toward Sage to calm him, when another strike nearby put him into a frenzy. He reared up on his hind legs and, much to my astonishment, took the ten-foot fence post with him as he pulled it cracking and breaking from the side posts. The next thing I knew the post had slammed me in the back of the head and threw me to the ground. My Ranger hat went flying and Sage was prancing around, dragging the post with him tied to his halter. Mike immediately went to Sage to calm him, and led him away from me so I wouldn't be trampled. I didn't pass out but I was dazed and my neck hurt. I knew not to move with a head and neck injury. Marianne got on the ground and asked what to do.

"Use my radio to call in that I have been hurt, that I am awake and breathing, but need an ambulance," I replied.

She did and then went to the Yavapai First Aid room to get the oxygen cylinder at my request. I told her how to turn it on and to plug in a mask and hold it near my face. I heard the sirens in the distance but was still too dazed to be embarrassed. Soon Ranger Kathy was at my side and asked how I was. I told her I thought okay, but would she take my gun and secure it for me? She did. Then the world came, including my Kent. I was placed in full cervical and spinal precautions and placed in the ambulance. They started an IV and I was soon at the clinic where Doctor Jim took care of me. He cleared my neck for fractures, but I had a whiplash-like strain. My left side hurt, too. On x-ray, my tenth rib showed a fracture.

Dr. Jim gave me this caution: "I have good news and bad news. The good news is your rib fracture is not displaced; the bad news is that it will hurt as much in twenty-one days as it does now."

I couldn't sneeze, cough or laugh without a sharp pain from my side for quite some time. I couldn't figure out how my rib was broken when I was hit in the head. It wasn't until I reported back to work a few weeks later that I discovered the mechanism. When I put on my body armor, it hit right at my tenth rib. My body armor snapped my rib as I was thrown to the ground, probably with my back arched backward.

It wasn't long before I was back in the saddle again, and continued to enjoy Horse Patrol and win all of my "discussions."

* * * *

Winter meant night shift, snow, cold and ice. One evening, a predicted storm hit the canyon hard. Cars were sliding off the road and there were fender-benders galore. All available Rangers were out on the road to make sure no one was injured, to clear traffic lanes to prevent more accidents and to keep traffic flowing. Why people chose to drive on a night like this was beyond me. The ice on the road was dark and slippery: black ice. It lulled drivers into thinking the road was clear because the ice was not easily seen. Once you hit the brakes and started on your chaotic ride, the black ice became apparent. I learned to accelerate slowly and to brake easily long before my stop. I received a call from Dispatch that Deputy Jim with the Coconino County Sheriff's Department was in the park on South Entrance Road and had come across a car accident. I responded slowly and parked slightly uphill of Jim's cruiser. We both had our rotator overhead lights on. In the ditch along the side of the road, I could see a sedan with several occupants. I stepped out of my patrol car with my warm trooper hat, jacket, gloves and pant leggings on. Once my Vibram-soled boots hit the pavement, my feet started to slide. I hung on to the door to regain my balance, and gingerly made my way to Jim's car and then to the sedan. Up against the pinyon and juniper trees, the car had its nose buried in the snow. This was a definite tow truck operation. I greeted Jim who smiled back with a "what-a-night" look, and he assured me there were no injuries. I said, "Great," and went to the car. Everyone had their seatbelts on and the driver said he had been going slow but had slid off the road due to the black ice. I recognized him as a local senior in high school and asked him what they were doing out on a night like tonight.

"Getting pizza in Tusayan," they all cheered with smiles.

"Well, not tonight," I answered. "This car isn't going anywhere tonight. We'll get a tow truck on it in the morning."

Their car was off the road and I asked them to stay put while I got his vehicle registration, license and insurance information for my report. Deputy Jim stayed to help with traffic control around our vehicles as I gingerly made my way up to my car. I wrote down the information and radioed my plan to Dispatch. As I made my way back downhill to the sedan, my feet began to slide and I slid toward Jim's patrol car. He turned around in time to see me slide out of control but, at the last second, to keep from falling on my butt, I made a motion with my arms and torso that threw me forward, onto my right knee. I skidded to a halt.

"Yowzer," I cried out.

"Are you okay?" Jim asked.

My knee burned and hurt, but he helped me up and I was able to stand. That'll leave a bruise, I thought.

I affirmed to Jim I was okay and, with my achy knee, made my way to the sedan. I returned the paperwork to the driver. We told them Jim and I would take them home. We helped them out of the car and to our vehicles and slowly drove them home. My shift didn't end until 2:00 a.m. and I couldn't wait. My knee ached and I was hungry and cold. I fell into bed about 2:30 a.m. and was asleep in no time. When I woke up about 9:30 a.m., my knee was throbbing. I looked at it and was horrified at how much it had swelled up. I got dressed and began the ten-minute walk to the clinic. Boy did it hurt. I thought about driving, but the clinic was so close.

On my arrival they took x-rays. The doctor came in and looked at me incredulously.

"You *walked* here?" he asked.

"Yes," I responded.

"Well, your leg is broken in at least two places with shattered chips in between," he answered.

I swallowed deeply as he showed me the x-ray. There was a fracture across the top of the tibia, the lower, larger leg bone in the area known as the plateau. It is the supportive area for the upper thighbone or femur to rest. The side of the tibia at the top had a triangular piece broken off with chips all around. No wonder it hurt, I thought.

I knew this wasn't good and I was right. I ended up having an MRI (magnetic resonance imaging) and surgery to repair the fractures and clean out the joint. I healed and eventually returned to work. My leg was never as strong and over the years it began to deteriorate, with continued running down trails with a forty-pound pack and doing my daily workouts. On July 22, 2002, I stepped over a log on East Rim Drive in the park. It sounded like a gunshot going off as my right knee exploded internally. It couldn't take it anymore. Again it was fractured, but this time so severely, the knee was off at an angle, a twelve-degree valgus. I literally crawled to my car and went to the clinic. They called my Kent to take me home after the poor knee was placed in an immobilizing brace and I was given crutches.

We followed up with several orthopedic specialists and each

said the same thing: that the knee was shot, that I would never run again, and that I could not do the work described in my position description as a Protection Ranger. One even went so far as to suggest that walking would be an issue and that I should look forward to a future at a desk with little physical activity. Needless to say, that was the first of many nights I cried myself to sleep.

The next year I was under the knife. Dr. Tim was an orthopedist I knew from working part-time as a nurse in the emergency room at Flagstaff Medical Center (I had received my RN degree years before and worked there part-time to keep my skills up while working full time as a Ranger at the Canyon). Dr. Tim was on the same wavelength as I. He would do the best he could to fix the knee and, with restrictions, get me active again. He told me there was little to work with to keep the joint as it was and that a Total Knee Arthroplasty (TKA) joint replacement was the answer. He put in a Stryker Orthopedics Osteonics Series 7000 artificial joint after cutting off the top of the tibia and the bottom of the femur. The artificial knee was cobalt chromium and the spacer in between was polyethylene plastic. I was officially bionic. When I returned home, I was placed in a passive motion machine that brought me to tears, and I had to ice it throughout each day. Kent took daily care of me and friends Jules and Marker came by to visit and give me positive feedback. My golden girl Shannon was a constant presence.

I worked hard in my rehabilitation. I knew straightening the knee was the hardest thing to accomplish. So several times a day I would sit on the floor to stretch and, with my knee out in front of me, I would place a hardback dictionary on the knee. At first I could only take about five seconds of this. Then I could take it for longer periods and eventually graduated to the massive *Encyclopedia of Insects*, to which my sister-in-law Kris had contributed articles and illustrations.

I worked with Tom, my physical therapist, and was healing well. Kent marveled that my leg was straight again. I set off the airport-screening device every time, but it was a small inconvenience. Then the day came when the Department of the Interior Medical Standards Board rejected my annual medical exam. Ranger standards are incredibly harsh, especially since we have medical standards and not fitness standards. You are not allowed to have a prosthesis as a permanent Protection Ranger. I did not fight the decision because I knew I couldn't jump and run for any length of time the way I could before. If I wrecked this prosthesis, there would be nothing to work with to replace it and they would have to fuse my leg. At least I could walk, mostly pain-free. My Chief Ranger Chris was very supportive. I received my retirement credentials after 21 years of service. Human Resources assured me I would get my retirement when I was 62 years old. I had a secure horizon but no career, and my identity as a capable athlete was also threatened. It was a very difficult time for me both physically and mentally.

For these past few years I have worked as an Adjunct Professor of Biology at Northern Arizona University and part-time as a nurse in the ER at Flagstaff Medical Center. I became a volunteer paramedic for the Tusayan Fire Department and taught Emergency Medical Technician courses for the community. I wrote, walked every day and continued to work seasonally as a Park Ranger in America's National Parks.

.406

One of the very finest resources at Everglades National Park is the birds. The Eco Pond bird walks are legendary for variety and sheer numbers. The hammock areas to the north of Flamingo have owls, kites and many other species. Vultures are very common. Both the Black Vulture and Turkey Vulture are found in the southeast and I have learned that the Turkey Vulture has a keen sense of smell whereas the Black Vulture does not. The Turkey Vulture finds its decaying carcasses not only by sight, but by smell, making it extremely successful. The odor of decay is very distinct. In South America, researchers placed dead chickens in the open and under brush. Both Black and Turkey Vultures found the carcasses in the open, but only the Turkey Vultures found the covered bodies. Playing on this knowledge, it was once proposed that natural gas pipelines in Alaska have the chemical that smelled of death, ethyl mercaptan, injected into the pipeline in a variety of sections. If there was a leak, one merely had to look for the circling Turkey Vultures up above. But the pipelines were too long and the concentrations of mercaptan varied. Besides, the Turkey Vulture rarely occurs that far north. But it was a cool idea. Mercaptans today are injected into natural gas, both in tanks and shorter pipelines, and leaks are detected by people smelling the stink instead.

One warm day I was driving south to Flamingo in Everglades National Park. There was a long straight section and I noticed in the distance something in the road. It was fluttering. As I slowed down and got closer, I could see it was a large bird with its talons through a rabbit carcass that was pretty much glued to the pavement with the combination of its body fluids and the heat. Try as it might, this bird tried and tried to take off with its booty. It would lift just a few inches, have its body all stretched out with its wings flapping, and then finally fall sideways to the pavement in exhaustion. I finally got within about fifteen feet of this bizarre scene and realized the large bird was not a Turkey Vulture, as I had assumed, but a magnificent Southern Bald Eagle. I turned off the ignition and stepped out of the car with my camera. At this point, the eagle was trying to slip its talons out of the prey and as it did so, I snapped a few photos. It finally released its hold and took off to the south.

Eagles could be seen from the breezeway that linked the Visitor Center to the concessions buildings at Flamingo. They often perched on signs and a few occupied the small keys or mangrove islands that dotted Florida Bay. The eagles were accompanied by a variety of egrets, herons, skimmers and rare flamingoes. I often gave bird talks from the breezeway where it was easy to see all of the birds. It was a great venue to instill in visitors the importance of preserving habitat so that all of these species would persist into the future.

On one such occasion, I was in the last few minutes of my talk, wrapping up what we had seen and reinforcing the preservation message. A tall man with salt and pepper hair and very broad shoulders joined the group. He looked familiar, but I couldn't place him. Heads began to turn toward him as whispers spread through the group. Strangely, it was mostly the guys who really stared at the newcomer. After the talk, most walked away, the men still glancing at the tall gentleman who approached me.

"Did I miss the bird talk?' he asked.

"I just finished up, but it's my prep time and I'd be glad to spend some time and give you a recap," I replied.

"Great," he answered.

For the next half hour we strolled on the breezeway, talking birds and ecology. He was remarkably knowledgeable about the birds and the local environment. He said he lived on Marathon Key and really loved it in South Florida. I told him about my summers in Sequoia National Park and he said he would love to visit. I told him I could send him some brochures, and he said that would be great. As I got my pen and notebook out of my pocket, it finally dawned on me who this man was. The small cadre of folks who had hovered a respectful distance away reinforced it. I then wrote down Ted Williams' address and promised to send him information on the parks. He shook my hand and again thanked me for the extra time and insight into the birds. He then walked over to the hovering baseball fans and spoke to them.

I am a huge baseball fan and while it was out of context, I appreciated meeting the last baseball slugger to hit an over .400 batting average, .406. The next summer I sent him the Sequoia brochures and he wrote back. Everyone loves the National Parks.

Heart Park

■ Sequoia National Park

"It's not the tallest, or the widest, or even the oldest living thing ...but it is the largest!" I exclaimed.

I was standing in front of the General Sherman Tree, the largest living single organism on earth. With 52,500 cubic feet of wood, it could make over seventy-five five-room houses from the lumber contained in its trunk alone. I don't know how many times I had given this talk. I had been giving naturalist walks, talks and evening programs in the Giant Forest since I first started as a seasonal Ranger Naturalist in 1979. After eleven summers, I became a permanent Ranger in another park and, for over a decade, visited my beloved Sierra yearly to hike and back-pack and see friends.

When I first worked for the U.S. Forest Service in the Sierra National Forest, I visited the adjacent national parks at every opportunity. Yosemite, Kings Canyon and Sequoia were parks I had camped in as a kid with my family, and they still drew me close. One spring visit as an adult, I camped at Dorst Campground in Sequoia and went on a walk with Ranger Dave.

Ranger Dave was a fixture in Sequoia National Park, having worked there seasonally for decades. I was fascinated at how he was able to bring the forest to life through great stories. After the walk, I asked him about the epiphytes – in this case lichens – in the trees. He explained with enthusiasm and then commented that not too many visitors asked about epiphytes. I explained I was working on my Masters degree at California State University at Fresno. Our short visit went on for several hours and, afterwards, he offered to write a letter of reference for me for the Ranger Intake Program. I was flabbergasted and flattered. Ranger Dave wrote the letter, but I didn't get the position.

I was so inspired that I applied for a seasonal position at Yosemite and Sequoia National Parks for the summer. I was on pins and needles, hoping for a job offer. At Fresno State I shared a lab with Dick, an easy-going tall young man who was also in graduate school. Then on the same day, I received offers from both parks. It was an easy decision; I picked Sequoia. It was the park my family had visited the most, and I was always drawn to its magnificent backcountry and Big Trees. I couldn't wait to tell Dick, and I went on and on about how great it would be.

He finally said, "So, you'll be working for my dad."

It then clicked. Dick's last name was the same as Sequoia's Chief Naturalist. I never put the two together and chastised Dick for not telling me sooner as he laughed and laughed.

I loved being a Ranger Naturalist at Sequoia. I was stationed at Lodgepole and went from there to the Giant Forest and even worked with Ranger Dave at Dorst. I learned so much. Over time, I gave many different walks, talks and evening programs, and even performed living history, where I dressed as a character from the past to bring it to life. I liked to tell folks that the Sierra was in my blood and, later, when I was working at other parks, would always have to return to get my "granite fix." Sequoia was my first and most cherished park in which to work ... it became my "heart park."

There are not many Rangers who do not have a heart park. It is often their first, but not always. I knew it was a privilege to be at Sequoia. Even though I lived in a rickety old cabin and slept outside on a porch, and paid rent and utilities for government housing, it was home. The friendships I formed there were life-long. We had potlucks and played volleyball and went hiking together. We vented, lamented and laughed together. Season after season I returned and felt complete in my heart park.

But seasonal work was not conducive to relationships. You have to move after the season is over and get another job in another winter park or, a job in the "real" world. I went to graduate school, worked as a city paramedic, and worked in some winter parks, but I always returned to Sequoia in the summer. When I finally met my husband-to-be Kent in Death Valley, we knew we belonged together. The following summer, I returned to Sequoia and felt incomplete. The winter after, I returned to Death Valley and, after a time, Kent and I decided to stay together. So when Kent received a job offer to become the Fire Chief at Grand Canyon, I went with him. But I went back to Sequoia and the Sierra every summer to get my "granite fix." I loved to hike and to explore and backpack. But one of my most rewarding hikes was in Africa.

* * * *

I was closing in on three months in Africa, exploring the natural history. I had spent time in Kenya, Rwanda, and escaped during a coup from Burundi. In Tanzania, I set my sights on climbing Mount Kilimanjaro with seven others. This was when there were still glaciers on the quiet volcano. I had first seen Kili, as the tallest mountain in Africa was locally called, from Amboseli National Park just over the border in Kenya. The snow and glaciers glimmered in the light as elephants, hyenas and zebras filled the foreground. But I also learned that the political differences between the two countries were felt across the border. Kenya was fairly stable and tourist-oriented. It had well-established national parks and programs in place for their conservation.

Tanzania had seen decades of upheaval. There were far fewer tourists, the infrastructure was poorer and the economy woeful. Tanzania had allowed the clear cutting of the forest on the north slope of Kili. Instead of having a watershed with trees to soak up the runoff, the water rushed down the mountain to the north. It ignored the invisible country boundary and entered Amboseli National Park in the adjacent country of Kenya, where it lifted the water table. This, in turn, killed the Yellow-Fever Acacia trees and changed the ecosystem so dramatically, that herds of elephants and other animals were impacted to the point where they moved to other areas or died off.

But now, five women and two men in our group were ready to climb. We had spent a short time in the capital of Arusha. There were some large hotels but also a tremendous amount of poverty. I managed to find a bar of chocolate for sale and a hand-drawn t-shirt that said, "I climbed Mt. Kilimanjaro." The currency was Tanzanian shillings. At 100 Tsh, the shirt cost about one U.S. dollar. There were no others t-shirts that I could find, but its homemade appearance and crude drawing had an appeal.

It was not as difficult or as expensive to get permits to climb Kili in the 1980s as in later decades. We drove through the misting day, never seeing the mountain until we arrived at the Kibo Hotel in Marangue. There, we paid to set up our tents on the grounds among banana plants and tall trees. There was another climbing group camped there who had just returned. They said of the fourteen in their group that went up, five did not make it, and all suffered from altitude sickness. We later saw a man strapped to a chair being carried down the mountain with bandages over his eye. Apparently, he was suffering from snow blindness. It was December, but there are no real seasons on the equator. The altitude made the snow a year-round force to be reckoned with. I would find out later just how fierce it could be.

In the old hotel, we read the plaques and gaped at the flags and photos from decades of climbers. I met a gal from Michigan who said she had turned back because the snow was waist deep on the summit. While small doubts crept into my brain about climbing to over 19,000 feet, I was still excited about the challenge.

I slept outside, with my mosquito net tied to the truck and draped over my cot. By this time I was fairly used to the night sounds of Africa and slept well. The next day, we hired a guide among the Chagga natives, named Siara. He was a head guide and said he had been up Kili over 700 times. He was 44 years of age, had eight kids and three grandkids. Siaska, one of my traveling companions, was from the Netherlands. We went to the market with Siara to purchase food for the climb. One of the many things I learned in Africa was the correct way to purchase meat. You never bought hanging meat. It was difficult to tell how long it had been there and the generations of fly eggs and maggots in the meat would only be discovered when you were ready to eat. No, if you didn't see the animal killed and butchered, you didn't buy it.

We picked out a small, bony cow and watched it prepared for us. The meat was wrapped in cloth, as there was no refrigeration. Then we went to the open-air market and bought onions, tomatoes, small potatoes, carrots, cabbage and rice. You also learn in Africa never to chew the rice with gusto. There was so much gravel mixed in with the rice, it would grind your teeth and possibly even break a tooth. We returned with our larder to the encampment where we found over sixty young and old men standing by, ready to be chosen. The bartering began as each man pleaded and Siara would point and choose the porters for our trip. He picked ten porters and five porter guides, and then Siara gruffly told the others to go away.

I hiked to a beautiful waterfall with two others on our trip, John and Yvonne, both from England. We found ourselves at a local village. They offered us a calabash and I took a sip of the potent liquid inside. It was banana beer. I passed on any more, but the others drank it with difficulty, pronouncing it "horrible." Their lips were covered with seeds, and it looked like they had kissed the bottom of a birdcage.

That night I was so excited I didn't sleep well. I saw Orion, bright in the sky above, and heard dogs barking in the distance. In the morning, the porters arrived and took our gear, pots, pans and food, and put it on their heads and started the hike up. Each carried about 65 pounds! We had our daypacks and cameras. What a luxury to climb with only 15 pounds. I even paid a porter 50 Tsh (about 50 cents) to carry a walking stick for me. I wouldn't need it now, but I was told I would be grateful for it later. The trail began as an old rough road that turned into a hiking trail with large trees canopied overhead. Vines dangled down and we half expected Tarzan at any minute. Our five-day plan was to hike from hut to hut each day, starting at 6,000 feet and hitting the top at over 19,000 feet and then back down. Each day there was a change in vegetation as we climbed higher and higher. It became more open and exotic, passing Giant Lobelia and groundsel, until there were only tiny alpine-like flowers and shrubs. We climbed slowly and became acclimatized each day. The summit lived in a cloudbank and it didn't show its small side crater, Mawenzi, until the day before the ascent. Every night it became icy and cold and we woke to frost on the ground and vegetation. The huts were fine, with bunks in a shared room at each nightly stop. From Horombo Hut at over 12,000 feet we finally saw the glistening top of Kili in the sunset with an incredible alpine glow.

By the day of the final ascent, we had walked through newly fallen snow to a cement structure at 15,500 feet. It was barren and cold and we all began to feel the effects of altitude. It was hard to think about eating, and some were having a hard time keeping food down. Sacha (who was from Canada), Siaska and I all had headaches, but we weren't puking our brains out like the other four.

I lay in the top bunk, just inches from the ceiling. I thought about taking a Diamox tablet a friend recommended to prevent cerebral edema. But it was also a diuretic and I didn't want to have to urinate frequently in the subfreezing temperatures, so I opted not to. I had a truly splitting headache and did not have any supper and only sips of water. We were scheduled to get up after midnight and head up to the summit in time to greet the sunrise. Throughout the evening, lightning and thunder rolled through our little hut. I never slept and by 11:45 p.m., I sat up in the bunk to try to relieve the headache.

Just after midnight, Siara came into our hut with a cup of tea for each and some stale biscuits. He told us to only have one cup of tea each. Then we dressed and took turns going outside to the outhouse. It was dark and cold and snowing. In fact, the snow was blowing sideways in blizzard-like conditions. I had a bite of chocolate and read on my thermometer that it was below freezing in the hut. I had brought hiking boots and my down jacket and hood just for this climb. With all of my layers and gaiters and walking stick, I was warm and ready to go. Siara returned with four other porter/guides. He had two lit kerosene lanterns that flickered through their glass chimneys.

We walked single file as we started out in the dark, each walking in the steps of the person ahead of us. It was fairly flat at first, but then became steeper and steeper. The trail soon disappeared and it was difficult to locate it in the blizzard and snowfall. We began small individual traverses, going steeply up the cinder-coated side of the volcano in the dark. I heard retching behind me and a couple were seen to turn around and head back to Kibo hut. Soon we were all spread out. There were so few of us that we each ended up having our own guide. My guide Alfred and I kept a steady but *polé, polé* (slow) pace. There is a lot less oxygen at 19,000 feet and I began to question if I would make it. I had only a headlamp and Alfred had a flashlight. Alfred knew very little English and was dressed in sneakers, a windbreaker and pants. The lightning flashes lit the whole mountain up and when it reflected off the snow it was like getting a camera flash right in the eyes. About halfway up the mountain, the snow stopped briefly and the stars shone through the opening in the clouds ... then they were gone as the clouds closed again. I struggled to go straight up the side of the mountain without any trail. It was very difficult and I finally sat for a break. Alfred was immediately at my side and pointed with his light under an overhang. I got up and we made our way to Hans Meyer's Cave. We crawled into the alcove and it was heaven getting out of the wind. No one else was there. There were icicles hanging from the ceiling and broken on the ground mixed with trash left by prior occupants.

Alfred reached over and rubbed my hands after I took my gloves off.

"Come on mama, come on sister, you make it, you make it," he implored.

Despite teaching him my name, repeatedly, he always called me mama or sister. I never heard any other English from him except for "yes" and "no." I shared my chocolate and gorp with him and gave him my glove liners and wool cap. His hands and head had been bare. I knew I was at the halfway point and it would be so easy to turn around. But Alfred kept imploring me. I think he knew if he got me to the top, I would be very thankful and reward him accordingly. Then I remembered that damn one dollar t-shirt I bought in Arusha. If I didn't make it to the top, I could never wear that shirt. That did it. I smiled and indicated we would go on. His ear-to-ear grin split his face wide open and we exited the little cave to continue the trek. The snow packed under my boots and I had to stomp and scrape them. We were not hiking on the trail and the scree under the snow made the ground move. I was slow, but persistent. Whenever I stopped, Alfred was there to brush the snow off me and to encourage me,

"Come on mama, come on sister, you make it, you make it."

I caught my breath every few steps and kept on. I had tied my bandana around my mouth and nose, steaming up my glasses, but it was so cold. At about 5:00 a.m. it began to get light. I pictured all of my relatives, and a WWII song my Mom used to sing kept repeating in my head:

"You gotta get up, you gotta get up, you gotta get up in the morning."

Then, above us appeared Sacha. Her porter was leading her down the slope. She told me she had made it, but the snow was waist deep. It took me another hour to make it to the top. Because we were off trail, we ended up climbing over five-foot boulders and overhangs. To this day, I am not quite sure how I did it, but I would not have made it without Alfred. At the top was a pole with a sign. The snow was very deep, up to my chest in one area, and not too many had broken the drifts for us. I showed Alfred how to work my camera, and he took a photo of me on top of Mt. Kilimanjaro in a blizzard. By some miracle, that photo came out.

We meandered around a bit, trying to wait out any possible view. At one point I think I saw across the crater, but was not sure. Finally, the wind and the cold were so severe; we knew it was time to go. It was turning into a whiteout. Others had dug out the register, and I found it and signed it. Then we started down, straight down. It was steep and precarious, but Alfred and I linked arms and took giant steps and felt the snow and scree slide under us. I felt like the group in the poppy fields in the *Wizard of Oz*, peeling down the mountain, picking up speed in the snow and the wind and the drifts. My legs got rubbery as exhaustion set in and we stopped for gorp. In seventy-five minutes we were back at the overhang. In the daylight I could see a bronze plaque commemorating Hans Meyer's Cave. We continued on. Then Alfred began to get abdominal cramps and weakened. Suddenly I realized the man I depended to get me off this volcano might not be there for me. We stopped and I gave him some water and more chocolate and held him tight to try to warm him. That seemed to help and we linked arms again and held each other up as we careened down the mountain. We were soon overtaken by two others in our group and their guide. Thomas was supporting Siaska as Alfred supported me; or rather we were supporting each other at this point. Within a half hour we all stumbled into Kibo Hut, exhausted.

We weren't there long. "Climb high, sleep low," is a climbing mantra that helps prevent altitude illnesses like cerebral edema and pulmonary edema. We gathered our few belongings, had some tea and bananas, and started down to Horombo Hut at over 12,000 feet. Soon the snow was merely lace on the landscape and the wind had fallen to a breeze. But as we descended, it began to rain quite hard and the trail became a raging torrent. We staggered the six miles to Horombo and arrived there soaking wet. There was a bowl of stew to greet us, along with some tea. After a light meal, we all crawled into bed for a few hours then up at 5:00 p.m. for supper. I went outside and the skies had cleared. I could see from the snows of Kilimanjaro to the Blue Mountains of Amboseli National Park in Kenya. I watched an incredible sunset with the others, and then slept deeply through the night.

The walk out was completed the next day and we all celebrated at Kibo Hotel. We were given climbing certificates and taught the song of the mountain, "Kilimanjaro." I gave

Alfred my gloves and wool watch cap, flashlight batteries, socks, a big tip and a big hug. I was truly overwhelmed by my sense of accomplishment, but also by Alfred's true sincerity and caring manner. When I wrote down Alfred's name in my logbook and pointed to him, he shook his head, pointed to himself and said "Hafrey." I finally learned his *Chagga* name. I had some awesome blisters on my feet and my down jacket was soaked, but I had made it!

But the story was not quite over. I managed to get a ride to Kilimanjaro International Airport the next day for my flight north to Nairobi. The airport was a single building and single airstrip. When I went inside, I went to the counter to check in, but it appeared deserted. I finally found someone who said my flight had been cancelled and there would not be another for two days. Oh no. This would mean I might miss my flight home to the States! I had to get there tonight.

I got a ride into Arusha and was told by a woman at a hotel that it was too dangerous to go by ground to Nairobi at night. "It's only three hours," I thought. Then I found a man who could "help to arrange things." I paid him to take me to the bus station, but the last bus for Nairobi had already left, and so he left me there. Soon I was surrounded by three men who were arguing over me. I figured out in my little Swahili that they could take me to Nairobi, for a price. I settled on a man who had a maroon Peugeot with a hatchback and a cracked windshield. I looked in the car and there were already twelve people in a five-passenger car. I started to back out, but the driver took a woman out of the front seat and put my bag there to show the seat was mine. I felt guilty, and so I bought a bunch of bananas and shared it with the dozen in back, cracked open my last chocolate and received lots of smiles. I climbed in, noted there were no seatbelts, and laid my bag on my lap. We headed north at a high rate of speed. At one point I saw the needle at 140 kph! We slowed through Masai Villages, braked for cattle and saw an incredible sunset – but the smell of the packed humanity was atrocious. I had to have my window down a bit just to breathe.

We arrived at the border station at Namanga after dark. I gave my driver only half the money I owed him to ensure my bags would be there after I went to the visa station. The visa was $5 USD, but the two border patrol officers hemmed and hawed and found other people to help. I said I needed to get my passport stamped and handed my passport back to them, this time with two $20 bills inside. I quickly received my visa and stamped passport and was in Kenya. I paid off the Tanzanian driver and quickly found a ride to Nairobi, stuffed in the back of a hatchback with five other women. The driver was old and tired and, as he drove north, he would drift across the lane into oncoming traffic. When it rained, the windshield wipers smeared the mud, and I had no idea how he saw through it. We were stopped at a checkpoint halfway and had our bags searched. Then, only 25 miles from Nairobi, the muffler fell off the car. The driver picked it up and tied it to the top of the car. We limped into Nairobi sounding like a contender for the Indy 500!

A friend had made a reservation for me at the Meridian Hotel. The driver took me there and I was able to exchange traveler's checks to pay him. Phew!

* * * *

I have been fortunate to go on many hikes in many places. But my beloved Sierra will always be number one. There have been some obstacles in getting "home" once I moved to the Grand Canyon with Kent. What an incredible resource. Hiking the canyon is a pleasure, a privilege and often a grueling event. We used to say, "Only fools and Rangers hike the canyon in the summer." This was because of the intense heat. I would try to prehydrate anytime I had to hike or fly into the canyon for a rescue in the summer. We kept cotton sheets soaked in water in a freezer at the helibase for heat stroke patients. When the call came, it was added to our arsenal of treatments. But on one call we had very little time.

We had completed some shorthaul training, so the doors were off of the helicopter. The call came in for a woman who was unconscious near Salt Creek. It was an August afternoon, so we assumed it was a heat related emergency. We had our safety briefing with the pilot Jerry, and then Dave and I boarded the Bell Long Ranger and took off for the short flight. Jerry dove into the canyon from the abyss. The G-forces were impressive, but as we went lower in elevation, the oppressive heat hit us. We saw a blue dome tent with three persons outside on the open Tonto Platform. The nearest LZ was up a sixty-foot hill just above the tent, about 75 yards away. Jerry kept the engines going while Dave and I jumped out – a "hot" off load. We scurried down the hill. In the tent was an unconscious woman; she was being baked alive. As well meaning as it was to try to provide shade for a person with heat illness, a lean-to that provided shade and good air circulation would have been a wiser choice. This dome tent was acting like a Dutch oven and her heat illness was only being exacerbated.

I grabbed the end of the foam pad she was lying on and called to the others to help. We pulled her out and I yanked her shorts to her knees, placing her on her left side with her knees to her chest. Dave had already set up my IV as I placed a thermometer into her rectum . . . the most accurate of core temperature sites. There was no time for modesty here. I had a companion hold onto the thermometer end as Dave and I opened our personal water bottles and poured them all over the 28-year-old woman. We then had another companion begin to fan her as I started a quick IV of normal saline with the line wide open to give her fluids. Dave placed her on oxygen by nasal cannula, and got some vital signs. I reached for the thermometer and was horrified to see 106.2 degrees Fahrenheit. I hadn't even left it in long enough to get a full reading! Dave and I were on the same page as we implored the others to grab an end of the foam pad and start up the hill. We had been on scene less than five minutes. Jerry had shut down the rotors and was by our side, helping to haul this gravely ill young woman up the steep slope to the helicopter. We loaded her into the ship and secured her on the longboard. Dave made sure the others were all right to continue out on their own. We donned our helmets, put on our seatbelts and Jerry started the ship. I called a brief report to Dispatch to pass on to the clinic and was told an ambulance was standing by at the helibase. We soared across the plateau and made a long loop to gain altitude. The air rushed into and across the ship without its doors and began a massive evaporative cooling of the young woman. Despite our attempts to rouse her, she remained deeply unconscious. But she did have a gag reflex as she rejected an airway we tried to put into her mouth.

We were at the helibase before I even thought to look up, and we carried her to the ambulance and drove to the clinic. Her rectal temperature was now only 103.5. That was great news, but we feared the worse. With that high of a core temperature, the brain bakes and cells die. You don't want to cool a heat stroke patient too quickly, to the point of shivering. The shivering will cause an increase in body temperature sending the core temperature up again. It's a fine line.

She was transferred to the ICU at Flagstaff Medical Center and was in a coma for several days. She made it, but had some cognitive deficits and short-term memory loss. We hoped that would improve with time. So you see, when "locals" hike the canyon for pleasure, we do so in March and November, with cooler day temperatures and warm – not hot – nights.

* * * *

When hiking in the Sierra, it's not the heat that can be an issue, but the cold. I have been snowed on every month of the year in those mountains. I once heard that there is no such thing as bad weather, just poorly prepared people. I hike with layers in the mountains to guard against hypothermia. It does not have to be really cold to get hypothermia, just cooler than your core, and no way to maintain your body heat. Folks have gotten hypothermia with an ambient temperature of 65 degrees outside. When you hike, you generate heat. When you stop, the cold can sap your heat. So when you stop, you need to put on dry clothes, layer up, cover your head and eat ... replenish those lost calories. I know this and I teach this.

After I received my artificial knee, it was pretty devastating. So much of what I did was defined by my athleticism; my physical activity as a Rescue Ranger, my participation in sports, my daily runs and workouts for my job, and my favorite pastime, hiking. I was told by my orthopedic surgeon, Doctor Tim, not to run or jump ever again after my surgery. But he said I could walk and hike and backpack. I was bound and determined to do so.

I worked hard in recovery. My physical therapist, Tom said he had to rein me in so I wouldn't overdo it. I stretched and achieved a good range of motion, and I walked. I walked everywhere and my Golden Retriever Shannon walked with me. Kent would join us on his free time, but it was a constant goal to achieve capability again. My surgery was in September. The following summer, I returned to Sequoia National Park as a seasonal Ranger Naturalist for the first time in over a decade. I lived in shared housing and saw Kent only once that summer, as his career kept him in "the Ditch" as we lovingly called the Canyon. My best friend Mary Anne was at Lodgepole and we walked, hiked and backpacked that summer. By the end of my season in my "heart park" I knew I was ready. I had pored over the maps, sent a cache to Muir Trail Ranch, and was ready to tackle the John Muir Trail.

Mary Anne drove me to Yosemite and to the trailhead. I was going to backpack all the way south to Mount Whitney then go west on the High Sierra Trail and exit at Giant Forest, over 230 miles. I was walking home. My pack was heavy, just over fifty pounds, but it got lighter as the days went by. I was no longer fast, but persistent, just like climbing Kili. I had walking sticks that helped tremendously and my slower pace allowed me to really take in the landscape. I had allotted three weeks for this adventure. Each day I got stronger and surer of my new knee. I had a sleeve brace on it, which helped. By the time I got to Muir Trail Ranch to pick up my one food cache, I was strong and confident. I received a lot of comments from folks I passed about hiking solo, and with an artificial knee. As I dropped down to Le

Conte from Evolution, the weather began to take a turn. I woke up to a drizzly day and a cold wind. I headed for the Golden Staircase that would take me over the highest altitudes of the entire trip with no way to exit for three days. I checked in at the Le Conte Ranger Station but Ranger Bob was out on patrol. So I pushed on past Grouse Meadow and up the drainage toward the base of the long ascent.

That night was the first night I set up my shelter. I much prefer sleeping out in the open and I usually shun tents. I am happiest when I can see the stars if I wake up during the night and breathe cold air while I am toasty and warm in my down sleeping bag. I had multiple layers on. I set up my little shelter with no floor – not even a true tent – in an open area adjacent to trees and near a stream. The next day I woke up to snow. The ground had about a half an inch and it was still coming down. The wind was blowing and the wind chill was considerably below freezing. As I heated up water for my breakfast oatmeal, I mulled over the options in my head, and knew this was the end of the line. It was September, a wild month when some of the worst winter weather had caught some unprepared folks in the past, sometimes resulting in fatalities. I was prepared, but I didn't know how long this storm would last. By climbing, it would only get colder. I had also promised my friends and family I would use common sense and make good decisions. I packed up and back-tracked in the snow to the Le Conte Ranger Station. I felt good and strong and arrived by noon. Now the wind was really blowing, but it was sleet more than snow. I sat in the lee of the small cabin and heated up some ramen noodles. Warmed and with energy, I started up the switchbacks to Dusy Basin. I was sure I would top over Bishop Pass and make it out. It was fourteen more miles, but I was the strongest I had been in a long time and my knee was doing great. After only a few switchbacks, I ran into a wrangler coming down with a string of mules to resupply a party. He said it was snowing up top and thought I would be better off hanging out at the campground near the Ranger Station. I thanked him, but kept on. It was a steep ascent, and I would hike one hundred paces with vigor, then stop and catch my breath, then climb another one hundred. I made great time, but the sleet turned to snow and the trail began to disappear. It was an icy crossing over one bridge, and I had to slow to keep my balance. Higher still, I thought about going back down to tree line and bivouacking for the night, but there was still daylight and I felt good. No one likes to lose altitude if they can help it. So up I went.

Within thirty minutes I had slowed to a crawl. I had a hard time finding the trail. I would occasionally see the clumped snow that had fallen from a mule's shoe or droppings from the wrangler's string and then keep going. But now I was really going slow and without realizing it, losing precious daylight. I came to a wide expanse, which was lower Dusy Basin, but by now, there was no sign of the trail, and I realized that it was getting darker. I pulled my dark glasses down and it was already beyond dusk. I had no trail to go up, even though I could see the ridge where Bishop Pass was located about a mile away. Tree line was too far below. The wind really picked up and the snow came at me sideways. For the first time in my backpacking career, I felt a disconcerting rise of fear in my belly. I began to question what to do, how to survive, *could* I survive?

The fear hit my bowels and I knew if I didn't do something I would soil my pants, so I took off my pack and perched on a rock with my pants down. I had a bowel movement. It then hit me that I was on the verge of panic and that I wasn't going to let it get the better of me. I wiped my bottom in the cold and quickly buried the waste under rocks I could see through the snow. I then went to a three-foot-high by four-foot-long embankment of rock. There was a pointed rock at one end. I wedged my backpack sideways at the other and pulled out my shelter. My hands were numb from the cold. I tied the shelter to the top of my backpack and the other end to the pointed rock. I tucked the right side of my shelter under rocks against the embankment and laid my walking sticks on the left side and then piled snow on them. I had an effective shelter that sloped from six inches at my feet to less than four feet at my head and was less than five feet long. I could not stretch out. I pulled out my Thermarest and sleeping bag. I already had my raincoat on over my down jacket, my wool gloves and wool watch cap on. Keeping my boots on, I slipped into my sleeping bag and crawled into the tiny shelter. I was cold and wet, and my hands stung. I propped my head and shoulders against the external-framed backpack and my legs extended to the bottom of the shelter. It was a tight fit. I had a little Photon light attached to a zipper pull on the backpack and I turned it on. It wasn't much of a light, but in that little space, with the shelter just inches from my face, it was a beacon. I turned my headlamp on and reached into my pack for my stove. I had half of a butane canister left. It was enough for the ten days left on my trip, but I needed it now. I turned it on low and the warmth lifted my spirits. I held my wet wool gloves over the tiny flames while I lay on my side and the ice turned to water. The drips sizzled as they hit the "Gaz" stove.

I filled my pot with water, and boiled it for sips of cocoa. I had put a Snickers bar in my pocket earlier and took it out for a bite. Dinner was served. I peeked out under the shelter, and the wind was howling, buffeting the small bivy and spreading snow everywhere. I reached up and slapped the sagging bivy to get the snow off. I realized I needed to conserve my fuel so reluctantly turned off the stove. It got very cold, very fast. I pulled the wool watch cap down over my eyes, pulled my jacket hood over my head and sunk into my bag. After an hour, my hips and legs ached for circulation. As I shifted, I realized my bladder was full. I tried to ignore it, but that made it worse. I pulled the sleeping bag down and my rain pants and hiking shorts over my buttocks. I shifted my bottom off of the Thermarest and let loose. A hot stream of urine ran over my inner thigh and outer buttocks and onto the ground adjacent to the Thermarest. I had tried to pull the ground cloth up as I urinated so it would be beneath it, and I think I was successful. I am not sure I cared at that point.

I pulled my pants and bag up and decided to light the stove for five minutes. I did the math in my head and felt I could light the stove for no more than five minutes every hour and believed it would last until dawn. I struck a match and it broke in half. I would have to be careful. I would have to have matches to light the stove and splitting them would be wasteful. I took the stub of the broken match and struck it and quickly lit the stove, singeing my fingers. I warmed my wet gloves that never seemed to dry, sipped the weak cocoa, and then reluctantly turned the stove off after five minutes. It wasn't even nine o'clock!

I tucked back into my bag where it was black and warm. Every now and then I would peek out and the little Photon light kept my tiny world bright and familiar. It truly chased the dark away and was a major contributor to my survival. As I tucked back in,

I reviewed all of my survival strategies. I was keeping warm, eating a bit, staying hydrated and working hard on my positive outlook. There were real moments when I thought that this could be it, that I would not make it and freeze to death. The idea that I, a Ranger, would die in my "heart park" was strangely comforting, but on the other hand, I did not want to cause agony to my family and friends. Then I realized it was September 19th. Tomorrow was Mary Anne's birthday. There was no way I was going to die on her birthday and leave her with that painful reminder! I looked out of my bag every twenty minutes or so and slapped at the inside of the shelter to knock the snow off. I stopped peeking outside the shelter because snow would pile in or be blown in and release the little warmth that I had. Every hour I lit my stove for five minutes, warmed my hands, sipped lukewarm cocoa and knocked snow off my shelter from the inside. I was awake all night long, thinking too much, but reviewing my survival strategy. I was not going to sleep, as I did not know if my exhaustion would allow me the energy to wake up. Twice more that long night I went through the sideways position to relieve my bladder.

Sometime after 5:00 a.m., I began to discern a bit of light through the shelter. I knocked the snow off the buried left side and peeked over the snow that had piled up. It was crushingly cold. I could begin to make out the white landscape and edge of the pass that continued east. I tucked back in and lit the stove for the last time. After warming my gloved hands, I ate the other half of the Snickers and drank the rest of my warmed water. I sat and reviewed in my head the sequence of events it would take to gather my things and get going. Hiking would warm me up, but if I took any extra time to repack, it could sap needed warmth and strength. I smelled a funny smell and looked over at the stove. My Nalgene water bottle had fallen against it and the plastic at the top was melting. I quickly pulled it away before the shelter went up in flames. I reached up and turned off my little security light that had lasted all night long. What a trooper! It was, psychologically, my best move to survive the night. Then I acted.

Moving quickly, I literally stood up and toppled the snow off the shelter and sent my pack sideways. I worked fast: turned off the now sputtering stove and literally stuffed everything into the top-loading backpack. I already had my boots on so I stepped out of my bag, stuffed it in its sack and strapped it onto the lower portion of the backpack. I used my knife to quickly cut the strings that I tied my shelter with. I didn't have the dexterity to untie them and it would take too long. I picked up every spent match and tissue. I was loath to leave any trash in my mountains. My urine-soaked ground cloth and shelter were all stuffed into my backpack without ceremony. I rolled my Thermarest loosely, strapped it on and paused to look around. I even took a few photos. I had made it through the night, now I just had to make it out.

I swung my backpack on and went to where I thought the trail would be. I had been over Bishop Pass once before, so I had a feel for the summit. The wind had blown the snow into drifts, some thigh-deep, while other areas had only about four to six inches of snow. I checked my thermometer. It was eight degrees Fahrenheit. I am sure it had been below zero in the night with the wind chill. Now it was crisp and cold.

I began to see some symmetry to the land and headed toward what I hoped was the trail. I walked through the drifts and traversed the slope, many times losing the path I thought might be the trail. I saw rabbit tracks with the larger hind foot markings leading the way. "What incredible survival skills they have," I mused.

As I walked and walked, I scanned the ridge and after a half hour made out a very symmetrical item. I headed for it. As I got closer, I realized it was the Bishop Pass sign, with the post buried in snow. I had arrived. I don't know if I would have made it without my walking sticks. My knee-replacement surgery caused some nerves to stop sensing where my foot is precisely, so an inch to the left or right of where I thought my foot might be could mean stepping off into a gully or twisting an ankle. On the descent, the drifts were deep, especially on the switchbacks heading down into the National Forest. A calm came over me as I trudged along. Not only did I know I would make it out; I realized it was now downhill all the way!

After another hour, I walked out of the snow and began to get warm. I persisted, but became thirsty. Within a few miles of the trailhead I saw day hikers. I asked a nice family if I could have some of their water and they generously shared theirs with me and listened with interest when I told them I had just climbed over the pass. At the trailhead, I was able to get a ride into Bishop and found a hotel room with a tub. I had to have a sandwich from Schat's Bakkery, so I cleaned up and went across the street. I called Kent to tell him I was safe and then called Mary Anne and wished her a Happy Birthday. She was so glad to hear from me. She said she had been chopping wood in her front yard at Lodgepole. She had been watching Tokopah Canyon and the darkening winter-like skies, willing me to be safe.

The next summer I ended my season at Sequoia as a Ranger Naturalist at the end of August. Mary Anne drove me to Bishop where I went back over a snow-free Bishop Pass. I hiked on and finished the John Muir Trail and the High Sierra Trail, logging just under 300 total miles. My new knee did just fine, and so did I.

"DAWG-A-REE-AH"

One of the many perks of working in national parks is the fun you can have in your front yard and your backyard. Canoeing in the Everglades, backpacking in the Sierra, and hiking in the desert are all great. You make so many friends that it's easy to go visit them in their respective parks to take advantage of their hospitality and their "backyards."

One winter season, I was working as a Ranger Naturalist in Death Valley. My good friend Mary Anne was a Ranger Naturalist up at Scottys Castle, also in Death Valley, fifty miles to the north of my station at Furnace Creek. A mutual friend invited us to Sequoia National Park to cross-country ski. So with a few extra days off, Mary Anne and I met at Stove Pipe Wells and drove to Lodgepole in my Datsun wagon, Lemonade. We weren't on the road five minutes when a clump of burros congregated and stopped in the middle of the road and I had to hit the brakes to prevent a collision. The drive was at least eight hours long and this was an inauspicious start.

By nightfall, we had driven over Walker Pass on Highway 178, past Lake Isabella, when a black wall loomed up ahead. Again I hit the brakes and swerved, this time to keep from plowing into a big black cow. From Bakersfield to Sacramento, Highway 99 runs in an almost straight line with oleander bushes and some concrete barriers separating the north and south lanes. It had been a long night of driving, and Mary Anne was curled up in the front passenger seat with her seatbelt on when I saw the lights.

They were distant at first, and then became brighter and

stronger. I called Mary Anne awake and asked her to look at the lights and tell me what she thought. At the same instant, we both realized it was a car. A car traveling erratically and at a high rate of speed southbound in the northbound lanes! We were driving toward a head-on collision with a probable drunk driver. I flashed my lights and pulled off the highway and onto the shoulder as the speeding vehicle plowed past. Our hearts were pounding as we realized our narrow escape, but we knew we had to call the highway patrol or that driver was sure to kill someone.

I pulled back onto the highway, heading north. Not two miles away was a rest area. I took the off-ramp and headed to the only telephone booth. Incredibly, at two o'clock in the morning, there was a man on the only telephone! Mary Anne quickly explained the situation to the man and he got off the phone as she dialed the California Highway Patrol (CHP). I could hear her side of the conversation as she explained the imminent danger of an erratic driver traveling south in the northbound lanes with a certain collision at hand. There was a pause, and Mary Anne turned to me and asked me where we were. She realized that she had no idea as she had been dozing until I woke her for the near miss.

"Where are we? The CHP wants to know our location," she called.

I had an approximate idea, but didn't know the name of the rest stop. I turned and found a wooden sign just to the right of the phone booth and read the name to her. She, in turn, told the location name to the CHP.

"We're in 'Dawg - ah - REE - ah,'" she exclaimed over the phone.

Then she paused. She had lived in California all of her life and had never heard of "Dawg - ah - REE - ah."

She looked at the sign, which had closely-spaced letters spelling: DOGAREA.

"That's not DOGAREA; that says DOG *AREA*," she said to me.

In great frustration, she now had to convince the CHP that this was not some big joke; that there really was a maniac driver on the road. After she hung up the phone, she stood next to me as I stared at the sign with blurry, tired eyes.

"The letters are really close together," I lamented. "You can see why I thought that the sign said DOGAREA, can't you?"

To this day, she still says she can't. ❏

Epilogue

It was a difficult transition from Protection Ranger to civilian; from having a career to picking up freelance, seasonal and part-time work to make ends meet. It was difficult to go from running every day to being told I would never run again. It was difficult being in a community where I once interacted with scores of people every day to currently seeing only a handful.

But life goes on. Changes happen and you do the best you can with what you have. I have had some interesting encounters. Some made me laugh while others kept me on my guard. When you are a Ranger, especially a Naturalist Interpreter, you are always greeting and smiling at people. Often I have found myself in a city greeting folks as if I still have my uniform on. They look at me funny and say "hi" back to me, most of the time.

But I have put many people in jail. One man who was convicted of murder gets out in a few years. One man who I arrested for arson and rape died in prison; his family found where I lived and left threatening notes. I am still somewhat on my guard. Sometimes I'm green in my awareness, or sometimes I am cautiously yellow. But there is a habit I developed a long time ago that I have not stopped. It's almost an unconscious act. I look at people's hands. I may not be able to tell you the color of someone's eyes, but I can tell you what is in their hands. It has always been what was in a suspect's hands that could harm or kill you. Wherever I am, I still look at their hands.

G L O S S A R Y

12-lead – an electrocardiogram of the heart that looks at it electronically from many angles. A myocardial infarction may be detected from a 12-lead EKG.

901 – code used over the radio to indicate a dead body.

AC – antecubital space on the arm where large veins can be found for establishing IVs.

ACLS – advanced cardiac life support which includes EKG monitoring, 12-lead EKG, and associated cardiac medications.

advanced cardiac life support – see *ACLS*.

advanced life support – see *ALS*.

ALOC – altered level of consciousness; a patient who is altered can be disoriented, combative or near coma.

ALS – advanced life support; medical intervention beyond the basic level which includes intravenous lines, advanced airway management, and administering medications. These skills are performed by Intermediate EMTs and paramedics.

Altered level of consciousness – see *ALOC*.

AMA – against medical advice.

apneic – not breathing.

Bauman bag – – a canvas bag used to encase patients on a backboard; often for shorthaul extrication.

BLEVE – boiling liquid expanding vapor explosion.

BLM – Bureau of Land Management.

BLS – Basic life support or EMT skills.

BSP – base station physician.

BVM – bag-valve mask.

bunkers – *see turnouts.*

called the code – to stop all efforts to revive a patient after medical intervention has been unsuccessful.

catheter (IV) – a sterile plastic tube with a needle in the center. The needle is used to enter the skin and vein and is removed after the plastic tube is advanced into the vein. It is used for the administration of fluids and IV medications.

CCSO – Coconino County Sheriff's Office.

CE – continuing education.

CHP – California Highway Patrol.

CO – correction officer.

coded – slang for a patient becoming apneic and pulseless; clinical death.

Code 3 – driving emergency vehicles with lights and sirens and as quickly as is safe.

Code 4 – okay.

command – in the hierarchy of the ICS system, the person in charge of the entire incident. Also known as the incident commander.

coronary arteries – the arteries that perfuse the heart muscle, circling around like a crown or coronation.

CPR – cardiopulmonary resuscitation.

CSM – carotid sinus massage.

cyanotic – blue in color due to lack of oxygen.

DOA – dead on arrival.

DPS – Department of Public Safety.

decompression of tension pneumothorax – see *needle thoracostomy*.

diastolic blood pressure – the lower number in a blood pressure reading indicating the resting pressure of the heart.

EKG – Electrocardiography, the electronic monitoring of the heart.

electrocardiogram – see *EKG.*

Emergency medical technician – see *EMT.*

EMS – Emergency medical services.

EMT – Emergency Medical Technician, a trained medical professional.

EMT-Paramedic – *see paramedic.*

epi – epinephrine.

ER – emergency room

ET – endotracheal tube.

ETA – estimated time of arrival.

flail chest – when trauma causes three or more ribs on one side to be broken in two or more places. A flail chest disrupts the integrity of the chest cavity making breathing inefficient and difficult.

FLETC – Federal Law Enforcement Training Center.

general alarm – an all call for all available personnel to respond to a major incident or an emergency. It involves radio tones, pager activation and siren activation.

Heat stroke - hyperthermia – when the core temperature of the body exceeds the body's ability to cool resulting in tissue damage and possible death.

HRT – hostage rescue team.

HTN - hypertension – high blood pressure.

Hurst tool – extrication tool that works on hydraulics and a portable compressor. It is also called the jaws of life.

hypothermia – when the core temperature of the body cools so that it no longer functions resulting in altered level of consciousness and possible death.

ICS – Incident command system; the organizational system used to coordinate and treat any large or involved incident or emergency.

ICU – intensive care unit.

IDs – identifications.

I-EMT – Intermediate (I) Emergency Medical Technician can provide advance life support by starting IVs, establishing advanced airways and administering some medications.

IV – intravenous is a medical access to a patient through a needle and catheter. Fluids and medications can then be given to the patient in their veins or intravenously.

Jaws of Life – *see Hurst tool.*

Jugular venous distension – see *JVD.*

JVD – jugular vein distension; caused when there is increased pressure in the chest backing blood into these neck veins. It can be a sign of pericardial tamponade or tension pneumothorax or chest trauma

LE – law enforcement.

LZ – landing zone, usually for helicopters. A helicopter needs a specifically sized area for the skids or landing gear to land safely. This is the footprint. The tail of the helicopter can extend beyond the footprint as it does not touch the ground.

MAST pants – medical antishock trousers use to constrict peripheral blood flow so that blood would remain in a patient's torso where needed. For years, the MAST, first named Military Anti-Shock Trousers then later Medical Anti-Shock Trousers, were thought to work by actually transfusing blood from the legs back to the torso, then keeping it there. Studies showed that the transfusion was minimal.

medevac – short for medical evacuation; it involves rescuing an injured person from areas difficult to access. It can involve a litter team, helicopter shorthaul or other means of evacuation.

medic – a general reference to any ALS medical provider.

military time – a standard for telling time that continues to count upward sequentially from noon to midnight by adding a number to the hour after noon and counting the numbers in hundreds, *i.e.*, *noon is 1200, 1:00 p.m. is 1300.*

Miller splint board – a shorter than average backboard that can float.

Miranda rights – legal rights of a person in custody to remain silent and to have an attorney present during questioning.

MREs – meals ready to eat.

MVA – motor vehicle accident.

mycardial infarction – MI is death of heart muscle and commonly known as a heart attack.

near-syncopal – having an altered level of consciousness but not quite loss of consciousness.

needle thoracostomy – placing a catheter into the thoracic cavity in the second intercostal space, midline with the clavicle. Upon removal of the needle, air from a tension pneumothorax escapes, relieving pressure on the heart and lungs.

nitro – see *nitroglycerine*.

nitroglycerine – a medication given to patients with chest pain in an effort to increase perfusion to heart muscle.

nomex – a special fire-resistant material worn by wildland firefighters and those who fly in park helicopters.

NPS – National Park Service.

OAS – Office of Aircraft Safety.

OB – obstetrics.

OC – oleoresin capsaicin (pepper spray).

OPA – oropharangeal airway.

operations – in the ICS, the person in charge of details of the actual incident or emergency being dealt with, such as fireground operations or technical rescue.

orientation questions – asked of a patient to determine if they know who they are, where they are, the time and events of the situation.

Paramedic – Emergency Medical Technician Paramedic (P) provides advanced life support including advance airways, such as endotracheal intubation and surgical crichothryotomies; starts IVs and administers the range of medications in prehospital care; provides advanced cardiac life support through EKG (electrocardiogram) interpretation and monitoring, and defibrillation.

Park Medics – see *Intermediate EMT.*

PEB – physical efficiency battery.

personal protective equipment – in structural firefighting, the turnouts made of nomex or PBI (a fire resistant material), plus gloves, hood, helmet, SCBA, mask and boots.

PIH – pregnancy-induced hypertension.

pneumatic antishock garment – PASG; see *MAST pants*.

pneumothorax – a collapse of part or all of a lung so that effective air exchange is compromised or absent.

prusik – a loop of small diameter rope that is secured to a larger diameter rope and brakes when tension is applied.

PSVT – paroxysmal supraventricular tachycardia.

SAR – search and rescue.

sats – oxygen saturation; a measurement of the amount of oxygen a patient's blood is carrying.

SCBA – self-contained breathing apparatus; the tank that structural firefighters wear to provide them with air when entering hazardous chemicals or smoky conditions.

SCUBA – self-contained underwater breathing apparatus.

shock position – placing a patient on their back with their legs slightly elevated to keep blood in the torso.

shorthaul – to hang from below the helicopter for insertion into a rescue site.

SNHA – Sequoia Natural History Association.

SOB – shortness of breath.

SQ – subcutaneous (under the skin).

syncope – loss of consciousness.

systolic blood pressure – the upper number in a blood pressure reading that indicates the pressure that blood is pumping through the system.

tension pneumothorax – a condition caused by trauma to the chest cavity. Air entering a lung exits through a tear in the lung and fills the closed thoracic or chest cavity. Eventually, the trapped chest air can squeeze the lung and heart to the side, resulting in death.

tone – a dispatch alert for a significant incident.

tone-outs – pager activation for a general alarm.

transport belt – a leather belt that is secured by a buckle around the waist of a person in custody. Their wrists are placed in hand-cuffs on the front of the belt. This is safer and more comfortable for a prisoner being transported for a long period of time.

turnouts – structural firefighter pants and jacket that are made of fire resistant material; also called bunkers.

V Fib – ventricular fibrillation; a fatal heart rhythm with no organized beating.

VIP – volunteer in the park.